ACTING

How to Get Started

FRANK CATALANO

Lexington Avenue Press

TABLE OF CONTENTS

INTRODUCTION
An Acting Career

Film – Television and Theatre as Collaborative Art Forms

Film, Television and Theatre are collaborative art forms, combining the written word writers, designers, technicians, directors, and actors. The collaborative efforts of all of these artists is presented to an audience within the interpretation, style, and creative point of view of a director. For this very reason, the creative process in producing such content depends on the clarity and communication of all artists involved. In its final form, the actor plays a pivotal role in communicating each medium to its audience.

Being a Professional Actor in Film –Television and Theatre

A career in professional acting requires an enormous amount of training and preparation to enable the artist to understand the creative process but also function as the main communicator of each medium. An acting profession is more than just going to work every day at an office, a store or factory. Many actors will state that they do what they do because they love it and couldn't do anything else. In addition, a professional actor seeks to create an established standard of exceptional creativity and superior quality of expression while getting paid for the work that they do. This definition includes performing in motion pictures, television, and live theatre earning compensation through union minimums or box office receipts.

Individuals attempting to establish themselves professionally as an actor will work at as many projects with or without pay to gain skills, credits and notoriety from casting directors and agents. These actors starting out, don't necessarily perform for the money they will earn and will more than often earn a living at other types of jobs. An actor starting out, is on a journey possessed with a positive state of mind for the future.

For actors trying to get started, the main focus of their journey is to get their first break. However, when the first break happens it is essential that the aspiring actor possess the skills that allow them to create what a casting director or director is looking for. This is why studying acting is so important.

CHAPTER 1

Why Take an Acting Class?

I want to take you back to a special moment that we've all had it where you were sitting in a darkened movie theater at a play, seeing a live performance or at home watching television. You looked up at the screen and you saw a particular performer playing comedy or drama and your thought was that you could do that. Do you remember the voice in your head that said: "You can do that! How hard could it be?" Then you followed that thought with,"I really don't know how I would get started. Besides it's how you look or who you know, and I don't know anyone" But the thought stays in your mind, and you want to know if I did do it, how would I get started? Is there a book or a course somewhere that teaches you what you need to do to become an actor? This book is all about getting started as an actor.

"I'm thinking about taking an acting class… but why should I? Lots of actors you see on TV and in the movies look like they're not acting when they play their characters. "I can do that. I just need to know how to get started and can becoming an actor help me at my day job? The voice in your head that tells you that you could be a professional actor and maybe a star, but you still must keep your day job until that happens. Maybe you work on-line in an office or home in a position which requires you to communicate with many kinds of people. You may have a job where interpersonal skills could be helpful but are not a requirement to be successful. But you still have a thought that you should give it a try and become an actor? The logical side of your brain believes that study of acting has no value for your personal life. You may also have the belief that acting is a form of pretending and within the context of life is the same as lying. People that ***act*** within a given situation are creating an action based upon a falsehood. They are using untruthfulness to achieve a desired goal. If ***acting*** is a form of lying, then it can't be a good thing to do because it is a deceptive practice. Unless you are using acting for a performance on a stage or in front of a camera, you are a dishonest person. Right? But before you make this conclusion, let's look at the definition of what an actor is:

Merriam-Webster defines an actor in this way:
An actor is one that acts: doer

One who represents a character in a dramatic production or who behaves as if acting a part

One that takes part in any affair

Let's take a closer look.

An actor is one that acts: doer

Would you agree that most people have a purpose in life and ***do*** things within the universe that they live in? Now ask yourself what ***you*** do within your universe? It may be something very important or as simple as waking up in the morning, walking the dog, then going to a place of work and coming home again at night. What is your function and purpose in your universe? To be successful, pay your bills and have a happy life, or it may be more. Having a purpose and the act of doing things to fulfill that goal is the fiber of our existence. If you were a primitive cave person living thousands of years ago, your purpose in life might be simply to survive the elements, hunt for food and reproduce. You would be the survivor, the hunter gatherer or spouse. However, changing technology, complex human relationships, and personal requirements achieving happiness is much more complicated than it has been in the past. Your existence might be composed of multiple universes which include a variety of situations, physical spaces and people that populate them. To survive, you might be required to take on a slightly different character within each of these environments. You may have specific character traits at home with your family, your job, school, and community which are totally different from one another. In one universe, you may be the leader, and in another just a silent follower. Depending upon the environment and situation, you could be either the star player or just have a supporting role within the reality of a specific universe. You might be a bit player in the role you play at your job but have the lead role when you are home with your family. Sometimes, within a particular universe, you initiate the action and in others you just follow along. Whether you have a large or small role in each situation, you should be the initiator of all that occurs in that universe?

Have you ever had a time in your life where you felt you were just like a passenger just being carried along with the events of the day, literally "asleep at the wheel?" You simply follow along with everything and try to react as you encounter it. You're like a supporting character in a play that serves some larger story that is going on about you. In the ancient Greek theatre, messengers often performed these functions. These bit characters informed the major players of past or future events that occur off stage. While we refer to these types of characters as "bit" they support the larger story and main characters. You might feel that way at your job or school that you are influenced by others but have no actual relevance to the larger picture. I have heard this referred to by some as "I am just a small cog in a very large machine." On other days, in a different set of circumstances or other universe (time or place) you are the mover shaker triggering the events. On those days, you are the lead character, you're strong, have lots of energy, and the story is either about you or puts you in the center of a larger framework. What you do or say has an enormous influence on the outcome and well-being of everyone around you. My question, then is, for the most important parts of your life, which role do you prefer? Being the lead character or a secondary character serving some larger framework?

If you want to be successful within the important parts of any universe, you must initiate most of the action so you can influence the desired outcome. If you want to be the lead character, you need to know how to create and play the lead character understanding the intellectual, emotional, physical, and spiritual essence of your role. Be the actor as a "doer" not a liar. But let's continue with our definition of what an actor is.

One who represents a character in a dramatic production or who behaves as if acting a part:

You behave differently within certain situations. You act one way online, at work, meeting someone for the first time. Another way when you are with your close friends, and still another at home with family. Your behavior within each universe defines who you are, what your function is and where you fall within the pecking order of importance within it. It's just like being a character in a movie or a play. In one universe you are the leader: in others the follower and yet in others just a bit player. Remember earlier, we talked about being the initiator within each universe that is important to you. You don't have to be the leader in every circumstance, just those instances which are significant in your life, and you want to influence what happens within them. In those significant settings, be the person who others look to for answers. Let that become your role. Also, not all situations, even if they are important to you, are ***about you*** alone. There may be situations about larger issues that you would like to see resolved in a specific way. You will make unambiguous choices about how you will "act" within this universe. For example, if you attend the wedding of a couple who are good friends, and your purpose is to be there to celebrate their marriage. The situation is not about you, and you are not the bride or groom. Your position there is to support the two people who are getting married. However, this doesn't mean that you must be a bit player in that story. Instead, rather than sitting by silently with your back against the wall, take a leading role in their celebration by acknowledging their union. You would congratulate them directly and if a moment came up, acknowledge them to the group. But don't make it about you. Make a difference in everything you do, even if it is not about you contribute when you can in a positive way. A note of caution don't just contribute because you read it here. If you have nothing to add to the situation, just be attentive and supportive to it. How many times have we sat through conversations of individuals who really have nothing to say? The words come out of their mouths but have no meaning. This type of contribution has the opposite result and takes away from the energy of the situation.

The specific protocols of a given universe govern the way you act. You wouldn't want to behave the same way you do relating to family members at home when you are talking to your supervisor. What is expected of you within your family universe is quite different than a relationship you might have with a co-worker or supervisor. Almost every aspect of your interaction is different. You dress differently, your physicality is specific, and your use of emotion and language complies with what is expected for that situation. In each instance, you become a specific character functioning within an environment and set of circumstances and act accordingly. In fact, everyone "acts" a certain way within the specific universe they inhabit because there is an expectation by others for them to do so. Could you imagine going to an appointment for a physical checkup and having your doctor relate to you the same way as a family member would? How would they do that? They might criticize you, call you nick-names or rap you on the back of the head if your health test results were poor. As they slap you in the back of the head, ***"Stupid idiot... you really screwed the pooch this time Johnny Boy, your cholesterol is over 200. You're a dead meat walking!"*** If they behaved this way, how would you perceive it? Would you feel comfortable about their ability to address your health issues? I don't think so. We expect every individual we meet to behave in a certain way within a given environment and circumstance. Doctors should behave like doctors; teachers should act like teachers and police officers assume a vocal stance and physicality that you would expect from a law officer. When a specific person behaves outside what is normally expected of them (out of character), we must immediately reevaluate our perception of them. That revaluation determines our response to what they do and speak. If a doctor behaves like a family member with a familiar joking vocal tone and physicality when diagnosing your health, we may question his/her findings. You might ask the doctor "What do you mean I'm dead meat walking? Was that a joke?" If the doctor takes a long look at you and then bursts into laughter and says, "What it means is you're going to be fine. I was just joking with you." You may like the answer better than the statement, but you still might question whether his behavior works for you within that situation. This all has to do with your previously held expectations of how a should act and our perception of the moment. The truth is we don't want our doctors, teachers, or law officers to behave in the same way that a family member might. We expect them to operate within the narrow framework of what is accepted behavior that is associated with the relationship they have with you within the universe in which you live. What about you then? How are you supposed to act in each situation? Would your behavior be the same in all situations? How would you choose to be perceived to get whatever you want? That depends on the specific universe you are in. Once you understand this, you can perfect and use this technique to communicate what you want and obtain it. Let's look at the last part of the definition of acting

One that takes part in any affair:

You are engaged in what's happening in your universe and will have invested energy in whatever is happening around you. To take part in an "affair," as used in this definition, you must be engaged in it and have a vested interest in how it progresses and concludes. You must always be connected whether you are active, passive or a combination of both. This doesn't mean that our engagement in any event should make it about you. It means that you participate in the event itself actively or passively. Sometimes we are "active" and lead and other times we are "passive" and follow and act as a sounding board for support to a particular solution. Sometimes we are both "hybrid." The situation requires active participation for parts of it and others where you may be passive and take a supportive role. But remember, which ever it is, it is not always about you.

Have you ever known a person who makes everything that happens about them? Close your eyes and visualize that person right now. Next, think about the last time you saw them. How did you feel? Did their self-centered approach make you anxious, bored, or were you happy to just sit there and listen? Placing yourself into the center of everything within an event and making it only about you, creates an obstacle to any sort of communication or resolution. It closes you down to new ideas and perhaps better solutions. I'm not saying you must either be totally "active" or "passive," you could be both at the same time. You should take an active role in your universe and become a player within it, but a player focused on moving forward or arriving at a solution. Have a sense of what part you are playing in the big picture without simply focusing on just yourself. If I were to ask what Shakespeare's tragedy ROMEO AND JULIET was about, would you say it was a story about a Nurse or an Apothecary? Although both characters were vital contributors to the outcome of what happens in the play, they exist solely to serve the main storyline about Romeo and Juliet. Life works in the same way. Sometimes you will be the lead character and other times you will play a smaller role supporting a larger story. The important thing is not the size of your role in the real-life affair; it is your active commitment within it. No sleeping at the wheel allowed… ever. Now that we have defined "acting," why should you take a class?

After all this definition and debate, you're still not sure if you want to be an actor. The great part of it is you wouldn't have to go to a job and work all day unless you were the star of a television series. You would instead move from acting job to acting job. When the project is completed, you would then go on to another. Each time you worked on project, (film, commercial or play) it would be with a different set of people. Each project will have new requirements and personalities for you to work with. In addition to that, you would have to go on auditions for new work.

Makes me think of the Walter Catlett song from Pinocchio:

Hi-diddle-dee-dee

An actor's life for me

A high silk hat and a silver cane

A watch of gold with a diamond chain

Hi-diddle-dee

An actor's life for me

It's great to be a celebrity

An actor's life for me

The illusion most beginning actors have about a professional acting career is that it is an easy way to make millions of dollars and live and extravagant lifestyle. But the actual career path of most actors is quite different. According to Michael Simkins June 2019 article in the Guardian

(Simpkins, Michael – 2019, June 15th *https://www.theguardian.com/film/shortcuts/2019/jun/05/only-2-per-cent-of-actors-make-a-living-how-do-you-become-one-of-them*

*A recent study by Queen Mary University of London referred to surveys that showed only **2%** of actors make a living from the profession and that 90% are out of work at any one time would be sufficient to have most aspiring thespians reaching for the scotch, if only we could afford a drink in the first place.*

Now, let's answer the question, maybe you are not sure about the dream of becoming an actor. You dream about making a lot of money and becoming a celebrity, but still not sure if it's the life you want to live. You enjoy watching theatre, film, and television but you are reticent about getting up on a stage or in front of a camera to perform. Maybe being an actor is just that, a dream that you will never act upon. So why would you want to take a class or a workshop for something you have no aspiration to do?

You might consider taking an acting class because it might be fun, a great way to meet other people or just do something on your feet which is different from what you do normally. If you are a shy person who is uncomfortable about the way they look to others, an acting class may make you feel more confident about your own physicality. If you are tense and have a fear of vulnerability in your relationships with others, taking an acting class will help you address these feelings as well. These are all valid reasons, but there is another incentive here that is more compelling and the most important. You will learn to communicate more effectively within the context of a character. This is what separates an acting class from a public speaking class. Acting is about creating a character and communicating a story and most importantly, how you are perceived by others. Let's call it the ***art of eloquence***. This is an idea that can be traced to ancient Greece and Sophists and has all to do with being able to communicate effectively to ensure a positive outcome of what you are trying to achieve. This is the Art of Eloquence.

“

Talking and eloquence are not the same: to speak and to speak well are two things. A fool may talk, but a wise man speaks.

“

Heinrich Heine

CHAPTER 2
The Art of Eloquence

What if you could develop a skill of communication and knowledge that would facilitate a successful outcome in everything you did? It would be like betting on a racehorse that you were certain would win a race. When I say skill of communication, I am not talking about public speaking skills, I'm referring to a capability much larger in scope which embodies a communication skill that would guarantee a successful outcome every time you used it. I am referring to the ***Art of Eloquence.*** What is the Art of Eloquence? The Merriam-Webster dictionary defines it as "***the quality of forceful or persuasive expressiveness.***" This definition would seem to limit eloquence to a form of rhetorical communication, but it is so much more. It is a way of perceiving and developing specific protocols governing your behavior within the world around you. While it is true that ancient civilizations like Mesopotamia and Egypt developed systematic uses of language and writing to advance their civilizations and standards of living. However, it was not the until Fifth Century BC in Ancient Greece that the Sophist idea of eloquence was elevated to a higher art form that would make individuals who practiced these techniques, the leaders of the ancient world. Who are the Sophists, and what is the art of eloquence?

Initially, Sophists were considered to be clever or talented men who could use oratory skills to achieve a desired outcome. This idea had all to do with a Sophist's ability to communicate effectively with influential people and ensure a successful place in society. The meaning evolved when Plato and later Aristotle altered the meaning by connecting it to dishonesty. Plato and his followers claimed that professional teachers such as Protagoras were not really seeking truth but instead were using eloquence techniques dishonestly to achieve victory in debate. Despite this criticism of being superficial manipulators of rhetoric, sophists speculated on theology, metaphysics, and the sciences, and were considered influential people in their time. Sophists were persuasive and were able to always achieve whatever they wanted. I am not encouraging you to say or do anything to get what you want. This chapter is not about how to cheat and get what you want. Rather, it's about developing a new way of thinking and behavior through the study of acting that will enable you to communicate more effectively and achieve the results you desire. If you were able to do that and do it well, you could make almost anything happen. What if you could encounter almost any situation and know with the outcome would be? It would be close to being able to tell the future. If you could develop these skills and use them to achieve a certain goal, that would not be cheating.

But what about the skill of acting itself? Why would you need to take an acting class to learn the art of eloquence? You could take a course in public speaking, learn the fundamentals of speaking in front of people, how to project your voice and gestures to get your point across. These are all very important techniques you can employ when speaking in front of a small or large group. But the art of eloquence is a way of thinking about face-to-face communication that takes places in smaller modules over an extended period. Public speaking is more about making a concise presentation in front of a larger group of people. The presentation should contain information about a procedure, tangible product, service, or idea. It is often used as an intellectual approach to communication, somewhat like a puzzle, which includes the presentation of a problem and then the delivery of a solution in a coherent manner that a group of people can understand. **If the art of eloquence is the way of getting what you desire, then knowing how to act is the delivery mechanism**. Acting is much more complicated than public speaking. It connects the "what you want" intellectually, emotionally, physically, and spiritually all at once focused on a single person, even if they are part of a larger group. When you act, you are connecting to an audience of "one" even if you are speaking to a thousand people all at once. Acting is personal. In return, each member of an audience connects with you individually on an intellectual, emotional, physical, or spiritual level. Acting is also different than public speaking because it is not just about how you speak to an audience; its connection is focused on the individual person-to person experience. Every individual who perceives your physical actions and listens to what you are saying will do so on a personal level. It's a personal communication between you and them that evokes a particular thought, feeling or belief. You want them to become just like you. You want them to think, feel, what you feel and ultimately believe the way you do. In the past, leaders like John F. Kennedy, Ronald Reagan, and Winston Churchill had the ability to accomplish this in person, on television or over the radio. They could individually connect with each person that experienced their communication as if they were talking directly to them. Were they acting? The quick answer is "yes." They assumed the role of leader, comforter, or inspirer. and connected to their audience in a believable personal way. You might be thinking as you read this, "If I am acting to make my communication to an individual or larger audience I never met before, am I lying? After all, acting is pretending to be someone or something you are not?" The answer to this question is simple.

Acting, is the portrayal of a created character intellectually, emotionally, physically, and spiritually within a specific set of circumstances and universe. If you are acting then, you are not lying but rather focusing on a specific truth within a set of circumstances and universe that your character resides in. Acting is more concerned with specific moments that are evident in a story or universe and has less to do with the general truths in the world. Characters in a movie or live play portray the reality of the specific universe they inhabit at a given moment in time. A man runs into a burning building to save his dog. He's not playing the fire or being a hero. He's focused on one moment, finding, and saving his dog. Acting teachers call this "moment to moment." You only play the moment you are in and not a general truth of the world around you. What does this mean? This explains why you have a certain character you assume at work and a quite different character you adopt when you are at home with your family. Often in class, students are asked to stand up in front of a group of 40 or 50 people. When they initially stand in an empty space before a group of people they do not know, they are physically closed in, and their speech is usually very low or measured. I ask them, "Are you nervous?" They quickly answer, "Yes!" Then I ask them, "Are you this nervous at home when you are with your family or friends?" They answered "No." In fact, they say they are quite the opposite. Why, then, are they acting differently? The quick answer is that they are shy in a new situation standing in front of people they haven't met before and in a space, they have never been in. All of that is true. But the real moment to moment answer is that they truly don't know who or what to be in this new universe and their behavior shows exactly that. Their physicality despite what they might say, telegraphs to the world that they are scared about many things. Among them, not being liked by others, unhappy with their perception of their appearance or fear of really letting people know who they are. You could see this a mile away.

I once met a stage actor from New York that told me before he was an actor, he was a mugger. Yes, a real mugger who left his criminal life behind to have a career on the stage. He was very good at acting in the moment and I asked where he learned that. He told me, not in an acting class, but in Central Park at night. He would walk up to someone walking and ask: "You got money on you? Give it up!" They would invariably say. "I don't have any money." He would reply to them, "Whatever I find on you I keep!" As he said that, they would place their hand on the place in their clothing (pants or jacket) which held their wallet. In that moment, he knew exactly where the money was. Their voice said one thing, but their physicality said another. I'm not suggesting you become a mugger to learn this technique. But I use it as an illustration of communication and acting in the moment. In that moment in time, the mugger needs to know one thing, **show me the money**. Once he knows its location on your body, he takes it and perhaps after that, get away quickly and not get caught. It goes on moment to moment if the story and universe lasts. Please do not try to mug anyone at home. This was merely an illustration and more about the idea rather than the specific act. I am not sure if the actor was telling me the truth.

Another example of moment to moment, in a theatrical stage play would be Macbeth's decision to murder King Duncan so that he may take his place. He goes through the pros and cons of whether to kill the king in this soliloquy from scene VII from William Shakespeare's Macbeth. However, at the end of the soliloquy, at the very moment he speaks of his "vaulting ambition" his decision is made to murder the king. He takes through the journey moment to moment and leads us to his final decision.

MACBETH

If it were done when 'tis done, then 'twere well
It were done quickly: if the assassination
Could trammel up the consequence and catch
With his surcease success; that but this blow
Might be the be-all and the end-all here,
But here, upon this bank and shoal of time,
We'd jump the life to come. But in these cases,
We still have judgment here; that we but teach
Bloody instructions, which, being taught, return
To plague the inventor: this even-handed justice
Commends the ingredients of our poison'd chalice
To our own lips. He's here in double trust;
First, as I am his kinsman and his subject,
Strong both against the deed; then, as his host,
Who should against his murderer shut the door,
Not bear the knife myself. Besides, this Duncan
Hath borne his faculties so meek, hath been
So clear in his great office, that his virtues
Will plead like angels, trumpet-tongued, against
The deep damnation of his taking-off;
And pity, like a naked new-born babe,
Striding the blast, or heaven's cherubim, horsed
Upon the sightless couriers of the air,
Shall blow the horrid deed in every eye,
That tears shall drown the wind. I have no spur

To prick the sides of my intent, but only

Vaulting ambition, which o'erleaps itself

And falls on the other.

Source: http://shakespeare.mit.edu/macbeth/macbeth.1.7.html

Playwrights and screenwriters create characters that function within the universe of the story that has been written. It is through the inner thoughts of each character, spoken words and actions that audiences formulate a perception of who they are. The writer creates a "position" in our minds and hearts about how we should feel about the character. Now, let's go back to our first meeting of my acting class.

The next thing I do is to have students answer three questions:

1. What is your name and what would you like to be called?
2. Why are you here?
3. Tell us something interesting about yourself that we can all remember you by?

Let's take a closer look at how people try to establish themselves just like a writer would do within a new group setting. The true goal of the three questions is to provide the student with an opportunity make an introduction to the class to establish a "position" within the new universe of the class. It is their opportunity to create a specific persona within that group. It enables the class members individually and collectively to define and evaluate the introducer as part of the group. From the presenter's perspective, positioning is the ability to ***"portray themselves as a particular type of person."*** Positioning is done all the time, either consciously or unconsciously, when a person enters a new group. Answering these three questions establishes, for the first time, who you are to the larger group.

The first two questions are easy. Well, most of the time. Stating your name seems straight forward. However, sometimes people want to be called something other than their name. One time a student asked that we say their name twice when we referred to them. If we didn't say his name twice, they would become agitated and insecure. Other individuals want to be known by a pet name. They would say my name is Jonathan, but everyone calls me Johnny.

The "***why are you here***" question is usually answered by most students by stating that they are interested in learning acting, want to be an actor, or often that they want to study acting so they can be more comfortable around other people. On one occasion a student introduced themselves and when he got to the why are you taking this class question. They smiled and said, "My shrink said that it he thought it was safe for me to be around other people now and I wanted to give it a try." At first, I thought it was a joke but then they insisted that it was true.

The real core question is the third one.

Tell us something interesting about yourself that we can all remember you by which goes right to the heart of creating a position or first impression within the larger group. The members of that universe whether it be your job, home, a presentation, or the public at large, will establish their view of who you are, your character, and intention. Think about famous actors and the type of content they do. Despite their desire to be versatile, they often find themselves doing similar roles because that is what the public expects of them. Many actors have succeeded in evolving from one public perception to a new one, but it is very difficult to reconstruct that first impression. Think about the golden age of Hollywood starts like John Wayne, Errol Flynn, and Humphrey Bogart. The movie going public expected John Wayne to be a hero, Errol Flynn to be a swash-buckling adventurer, and Humphrey Bogart to be a wise cracking tough guy. The marketing departments of the major motion picture studios created much of this The movies could do this because the actors were all under contract up until the 1950's and how to be in the films that the studio heads wanted them to be in. Now let's think about actors today.

The mega movie stars are no longer contract players do everything in their power to be diversified in the roles they play. They want to be diversified so they are available for the widest variety of projects. Even so, think about the projects that Tom Cruise, Wil Smith and Jennifer Lawrence have done recently. If you look closely, there is a pattern. Not because these people aren't talented and could do almost anything. What's driving what they do is public perception. Now let's get back to question three in an acting class.

Students answering this question can choose to be whatever they want to be known for in this new universe on a blank page. What an opportunity, right? However, most individuals, when provided with the opportunity to reinvent themselves, connect instead to something else that they perceive will be liked by the group rather than answering the question. It creates the opposite condition.

"Hi, I'm Fredrick. I'm here to try acting. Something interesting about me? I mostly get up late and just hang around all day… play Warcraft."

That gets a laugh from the group, but what does the class think about Fredrick? He's a slacker.

"(sigh) I'm Janice. You can call me Jan… I am divorced. My husband cheated on me with my best friend and now I am all alone. I thought that taking an acting class would be a great way to not feel so depressed and to meet new people."

What does the class think of Janice? Needy.

When given the opportunity to reinvent themselves, most individuals rely on the very things they want to get away from. They connect themselves indelibly to some sort of negative perception they have of themselves. When they are given the opportunity to create someone new, they go back to what they know. Also, sometimes they don't tell the truth because their self-perception makes them feel uncomfortable. They make up something.

"I'm Dara and am taking this class to get back into acting. I used to do lots of movies and television and then kind of fell out of it. Something you don't know about me is that I've starred in over ten movies." What does the class think about Dara? She was probably an extra in a few movies or just not telling the truth.

Hello, my name is Dave. My friends call me "Pretty Dave."

(He takes off his shirt, revealing a ripped stomach. Group applauds.)

I work hard at my body. I took this class because I think an acting class is an easy place to meet hot women. Something you do know about me. I was in a porno film once.

(Loud applause) What does the class think about Dave? Someone to stay away from.

We are all liars at one point or another in our lives but acting is not about lying; it's about finding a truth.

We all lie at some point in our lives for any number of reasons. We want to cover-up something that we have done wrong; avoid a certain circumstance or person; want to be polite not to hurt someone's feelings or conversely to help someone who is in need, or we do so for a perceived personal or financial advantage. But let's not think about acting as the creation of something false or a lie. Taking an acting class to learn the Art of Eloquence is not about lying to achieve any of these outcomes; it is about how you discover a truth to communicate ideas more effectively and ultimately get the individuals you share with to do what you want them to do. You not only speak the words; you also convey emotion, spirit, and physicality. Acting is not about hiding the truth it is about discovering the truth.

When you act, you are not lying or masking the truth to convey a character in a play or a movie. Instead, you become a truth seeker taking in all you can about the situation you are in and connecting it all to your own intellectual thoughts, emotions, physicality, and spirituality. The process is the same as interpreting and playing a character in a movie or a play. Actors playing a role seek the "truth" of the situation, the specifics of the character and the universe they inhabit; the only difference in your own life is that you are not in a play or a movie. It is ***your*** life and what you are doing is real to you. The art of eloquence is knowing how to communicate that reality to whomever you interact with and get what you want. But what does that mean to seek truth within your own life, and what do you do with it once you find it?

"Acting is an everlasting search for the truth."
Laurence Olivier

So, why not just journey to Tibet and climb to a mountain top to meditate away the clutter of everyday life and discover your truth? The answer is simple; it's not enough to know your truth you must also have the desire and capability communicate it to others and more importantly getting others to do what you need them to do to manifest it into reality. ***Knowing your truth is not enough; you must act and make it into a reality.***

Manifesting your truth

Have you ever heard the phrase ***you can talk the talk, but can you walk the walk?*** What does it mean to you? Cambridge dictionary defines this phrase as: "***If you say that someone talks the talk but does not walk the walk, you mean that they do not act in a way that agrees with the things they say,"*** Does this makes sense to you?

This statement in as it relates to the Art of Eloquence means that you must live your truth and act not just talk about it. It's like memorizing a wonderful recipe for a chocolate cake but not knowing the first thing about how to take those descriptive words written on a piece of paper and transform them into a delicious creation. Learning the art of eloquence is about your ability to manifest ***your*** truth and by doing so, enable you to get what you want. But what is your truth? Your truth is the totality of who you are now, where you have been in the past, and what you desire in your future at any given moment in time. It is an integrated set of values and protocols that you establish to get what you want.

Values represent those elements of your universe that have the most meaning to you. They are your core beliefs that make you who you are. We will discuss these in more depth later in this book. Your protocols are the means or procedures you will use to get you what you want. Your truth then, is the total of all of the values and protocols. It's the sum total of your present and past and where you want to be in your future. It is also a plan of a detailed procedure that you will follow to achieve those goals. This is your truth.

Your truth is your dream at a particular moment in time... choose wisely

Your truth is always evolving as you experience new people and things in your life. On so many occasions, people have shared with me their ultimate dreams of what they want to do only to find that these aspirations, once achieved, do not fulfill them. Why is that? How can a dream once achieved become so unfulfilling? The answer is two-fold. One, often what we desire is based upon false assumptions and perceptions. For example, some believe that famous people, being well known, are always happy and so they want to be famous and happy just like them. They like the idea of being famous and being known by everyone everywhere they go. However, once the dream of fame is achieved, they have a realization that fame it is not what they thought it would be. People who are famous have no privacy and are often hounded by autograph seekers and paparazzi. The dream of fame for some becomes a nightmare. But your dream may be more personal. Your dream could be to live amid the tranquil beauty of a tropical island in the middle of the Caribbean Sea. You visualize a life filled with beautiful sunsets and long walks on the beach. But after achieving it, you realize that the tranquil Caribbean setting is devoid of the technology and conveniences you are accustomed to in a larger city. Your dream of life in paradise, once achieved becomes something very different. You feel isolated and want to get out.

The second reason, a dream once achieved can make us feel unfulfilled because we or our universe has changed. What we aspire to at one moment in our lives (a result of our perceptions and protocols at that moment) may gradually evolve over time into something else as our universe around us changes. We constantly evolve as well, and as we do; we perceive our life and universe differently. These changes evolve slowly and are almost imperceptible in any given moment. They are best measured over time. What you wanted in your life a year ago may no longer fit within your priorities for a newer moment. Don't be alarmed, this is normal, and you can adjust as you go by creating new sets of priorities and protocols and of course new dreams to go your current direction. I don't want you to think that manifesting your dream will never be achieved because you and everything around you are always changing.

A great way of thinking of it is not as much about change but more about adjusting and becoming more accurate. Think of a spacecraft going on a long journey to a distant planet. Along the way, course adjustments must be made for the trajectory to remain accurate and for the craft to ultimately arrive at its destination. In a larger sense, your adjustments can be interpreted as a narrowing down process, where you constantly simplify (removing what is no longer relevant) and until you achieve what you have set out to accomplish. It's like peeling an onion; our inner truth is only that truth existing at a specific moment in time. However, there is an inner truth, one that exists at the core of our existence. As time goes by, we slowly peel away the layers until we reach a true connection and an understanding that makes us feel fulfilled. Please don't think of this as a bad thing. It is as it should be. Life is a journey that has many different beginnings and endings along the way. It is better to undertake the journey than just idly hope for a wish that may never come true.

The art of eloquence is the way of thinking, communicating, and believing which will make you the kind of person who is in a constant state of reinvention. One that is perpetually moving forward and adapting to the universe around them. You don't have to go on a mystical journey to the mountain tops of Tibet to get there. Instead, create your own mountain top. One that take with you to wherever you want to be. But where do you start? There are several steps you can take to begin.

“

Once you make a decision the universe conspires to make it happen.

“

Ralph Waldo Emerson

CHAPTER 3

You Want to be an Actor

How do You Manifest Your Dream?

What is manifesting mean?

Merriam Webster defines "manifest" in the following way:

Adjective

1: Readily perceived by the senses and especially by the sense of sight Their sadness was manifest in their faces.

2: easily understood or recognized by the mind: obvious. manifest. verb. manifested; manifesting; manifests.

Verb:

Display or show (a quality or feeling) by one's acts or appearance; demonstrate.

"Ray manifested signs of severe depression"

Manifesting your dreams is about taking those ideas, hopes and inspirations that you have envisioned about what you want to do with your life and your desire to be happy. Manifesting would create a process to transform those ideas and feelings into a tangible thing action or result. This chapter is dedicated to showing you how to do this.

Documentation – write it down

Place a piece of paper and a pen beside you. Close your eyes and sit quietly for several minutes and let the normal day to day thoughts about feeding the dog, going food shopping fade away. If you need to play soft music (no lyrics) that's okay. Think "peace" when you inhale and "calm" when you exhale. Let random thoughts flow into your mind. At first, these thoughts will be concerned with the "now." You will be thinking of errands you must make chores you must do at that moment. Then there will be a period of nothingness… your mind will be blank, and soon you will begin to fill it with random thoughts. There is no reason here… you may list all your elementary school teachers starting with kindergarten going up to sixth grade or the paint colors of every house you have lived in. But then you reach a point where your mind becomes blank. Right there, ask yourself, "Where am I now?" This is not a literal question, but a metaphorical one. It may not come to you immediately, but if you clear your mind, an answer will eventually come to you. At that point the universe will speak to you and provide an answer. The answer may be "I am in a rut, everything I do fails" or "I am thankful for my job, but it is something I hate doing but I am afraid to change." Then think about where would like to be in the future. Visualize it and say it aloud. See how it feels to say it. Do the words you have spoken seem natural or does it feel wrong. If it is wrong, keep exploring the way you state it until it is a perfect fit. Let the energy flow into you and the universe will provide. As it does, write these thoughts down. Make two lists, one positive for inspiration and one negative for obstacles that must be addressed.

Self-exploration and feedback from others

Make two lists describing yourself as you believe you are perceived by others. Be honest, what are your strengths and what are your weaknesses that need to be addressed. Then, ask trusted friends and (optional) family members how they perceive you and your strengths and weaknesses. Do this to get an understanding of your own "self" view and how in turn you are perceived by the universe around you. If you feel adventurous, ask people you don't know as well. See if their first impression of you is accurate or off the mark. See if any strengths or weaknesses are repeated from different sources. A word on strengths and weaknesses. You do not have to address every weakness that each person highlights. Try to see if one or more weaknesses reoccur several times. These will be areas that you will have to work on. Also, a reoccurring strength can really be a weakness that prohibits you from achieving your goal. How can a strength be a weakness? Anything that stands in the way of your achievement is a weakness. An example might be that you are a detail-oriented person, and this trait is mentioned by several people you talk to. However, if being so detail-orientated means that you strive for everything to be perfect before you complete it, you may never get anything done. Your strength for detail might prevent others from collaborating with you. In this case, being a detailed person is a weakness.

Evaluate and Prioritize

Now it's time to create a plan by evaluating where you are at this moment in time and comparing it to where you would like to be. This is like creating a map or set of directions from one place to another. Consider your evaluation and the feedback you have received from others. Using this model, create a new list of items you must work on to take you from where you are now to where you would like to be, what you need to do to move toward your dream.

Declaration – write your letter to the world:

Once you are clear as to what you want to do and where you would like to be, you must announce this dream to the world. You must put it out there in positive terms. Don't preface your dreams with negativity by saying "I know how hard it is to become successful in this world and it's all about who you know… but I want to… be an actor." What's wrong with saying what you want this way? You're already creating a situation where you will not achieve what you desire. Not everyone is perfect, and we all need to work and improve on things continually that can be articulated as well. Instead of stating the impossibility of your dream, solicit energy and assistance toward it. Declare aloud to the world what you want; articulate it and ask for help. The universe will provide. However, you must create action to manifest your dream. Don't think you will get what you want by just thinking positive thoughts. Thoughts are great, but you need action to make it all happen.

To find your own truth, you must formulate an idea of what you really want and then act to do something about it. This subject is worthy of a book all by itself. The idea that you can create whatever you want using skills you might acquire in an acting class may seem absurd. However, I can show how and why you should do this, but I can't without knowing you, have an idea of why you want a certain goal. Your inner perception of what you want may be on a very rudimentary level. As simple as a career choice, a personal relationship, or a major to study at school. It can also be rooted more deeply as a desire to find inner truth, peace, well-being, and happiness. For example, do you have a certain goal that you work on every day that was created for you by the expectations of your parents or friends? Even though you don't really want it, you accept the goal readily because you don't want to be criticized or feel forced because a friend or sibling is successful at it. You find yourself on a life-long journey fulfilling someone else's dream instead of your own. The "why" you desire is just as important as the "what" you desire. The clinical approach to your needs and desires can be explained by looking at a theory of psychology proposed by Abraham Maslow in his 1943 paper published in Psychological Review called ***"A Theory of Human Motivation."*** Maslow later developed his idea further to include observations of humans' innate curiosity and desire to acquire knowledge. He proposed what he called the hierarch of needs theory, which attempts to detail a person's desire to fulfill five basic needs: physiological, safety, social, esteem, and self-actualization.

Physiological:

The basic needs you require in your life including food, water, air to breathe, warmth when it's cold and the ability rest.

Safety:

Security of your body, family, having a job, good health, personal property, a place you call home and a feeling well-being within those elements.

Social:

Feeling loved, belonging, not being alone, friendship, family, and general belonging.

Esteem:

Prestige, feeling a sense of accomplishment, self-esteem, respect of others, confidence in yourself and, respect by others.

Self-Actualization:

Being creative and achieving your full potential. Being a success.

Now that you have a general idea of Maslow's five hierarch of needs components try to fill in your own values to find your "why." Are all five needs fulfilled or are there areas that you need to address? Certainly, it's hard to work on the advancement of your career or life goals if you don't understand why, you are doing what you are doing. Students often tell me they want to be a famous actor, but they don't have a reason that goes beyond "I want to be rich and famous." My question is "why do you want this? You may think that being rich is desirable because you assume that having money will solve all your other needs. However, if you don't address all your needs, and know why you're doing what you're doing it may not accomplish what you think it will.

Do I need or desire this?

Most people think about what they need as something that they would categorize is "have to have" and what they desire as what they "aspire or dream about having." Your needs for you are what you must have, and your desires are those things that you hope will happen sometime in the future. Merriam Webster defines "need" in the following way:

1: necessary duty: obligation *no need to apologize the need to pay taxes — Peter Scott*

2: a lack of something requisite, desirable, or useful *a building adequate for the company's needs*: a physiological or psychological requirement for the well-being of an organism *health and education needs*

3: a condition requiring supply or relief *the house needs repair. refugees in need of shelter and food.*

4: lack of the means of subsistence (see subsistence 2): poverty *The community program provides for those in need.*

And now let's look at ***desire:***

1: to long or hope for: exhibit or feel desire for *desire success knew that men still desired her*

2: to express a wish for: request *they desire an immediate answer. archaic*: to express a wish to: ask *desired them to reconsider*

Desire, while it is tempting to think about, will always take second place to need when we communicate with others. When people need something, they go for it. If they are hungry, they find a way to feed themselves and they do it quickly. How many times has someone said to you…? "I'm starving… let's get something to eat now." Now let's use the same methodology with desire. "I want to be rich and famous… I want to be successful… let's get started right now." What happens after that? The result is not as immediate. There are usually obstacles that must be overcome or distractions along the way. The desire, for any number of reasons, is put off to a later date or abandoned all together. You may start off strong, but soon you will find yourself being pulled away because you are distracted by what you believe you need immediately. Your needs for "today" will almost always take precedence over your desires for the future. The trick is to think of your desires as tangible actions that you must act on immediately, rather than hoping that they may happen sometime in the future after certain conditions are met. What kind of conditions? The little voice of reason in your head will justify not moving forward for any number of reasons.

Do any of these reasons to ***not fulfill a desire*** sound familiar? ***"I can't fulfill my desire because…"***

I first must lose ten pounds.

It's too soon. I will when I'm ready.

It's the holidays… after the holidays.

I can't do it on Monday, it's the beginning of the week.

I can't do it on Wednesday, that's hump day.

I can't do it on Friday; everyone is thinking about the weekend.

I can't do it on Tuesday or Thursday because everyone is so busy.

The "reasons not to do" list can be endless. It underscores and certain unwillingness to move forward from the comfort of "now" toward a future unknown desire. No matter how unfulfilled you are now, there is a greater fear that it could get worse in the future. So, you put off your desires with the full knowledge that there will be no immediate impact for procrastinating. You remain in the comfort of now and everything stays the same if you continue to hope. This complaisance is followed by feelings of self-doubt and acceptance to remain as you are. It all ends there, and nothing happens. Why? You don't think of your desires the same way as your needs. Your needs get addressed first. When you're hungry you eat and when you are cold, you put on a sweater… because the condition demands a result now. But what if you frame your desires as immediate needs?

It's all about now – the future always takes second place

When you desire something in your future, your immediate needs will always come first. Also, emotions and self-doubt get in the way for the reasons we discussed earlier. For now, let's make two distinct lists, one containing your immediate needs and then another containing your long-term desires. Next, put them side by side and find points of connection to what you need right now so that you can achieve your desires for the future. If you have no connections, then you need to reevaluate where you are and where you want to be. Your immediate needs, at some point, should facilitate your future desires. For example, you may have a need to attend college at night to get a degree. That need should facilitate at least one of your future desires. You need to get a degree now so you can become a teacher in the future. The lists should connect at some points. When you are done, you will have combined both lists into one comprehensive side by side list of immediate needs connecting to future desires. Check each new combined needs/desire element against Maslow's five general categories? Do they fit? Not sure, let's look at another example, of a job promotion. You combine the need to earn more money with the desire to be successful in the future. A job promotion will meet the need to earn more money, provide you with a better professional title, more peer respect, and a general feeling that you are successful. Which one or combination of Maslow's five categories would you select to get a promotion?

Physiological: A promotion would give you more money for food and shelter.

Safety: You want to make more money and feel safe about your future?

Social: Having promotion will bring you more friends.

Esteem:You will feel a sense of accomplishment and have more respect from others and a higher sense of self-esteem.

Self-Actualization: Being a success in the eyes of others is important to you.

You may believe that all of Maslow's needs are met if you get a promotion. But which one meets your criteria the most? Try to make a clear connection to which of Maslow's meets your criteria the best. Once you have established that connection, you will have a clear understanding of what you really want. Do that same process for every item on your combined needs/desire list. When it's done, you will have your truth. Now that you have that, it's time to put it out there. That's the hard part.

When you ask someone to tell you what they really want from their lives, they often answer in a joking way. "I want to be famous, live in a mansion right on the beach in Malibu and drive a red Maserati." The question they really heard was: "If you could get anything you wanted just by wishing, what would you wish for?" This is really an answer to a fantasy that they truly believe will never happen. Also, when they answer, they usually connect the idea of "fame" with being "wealthy." So, I clarify and ask them if it is only fame, they want or do they want to be rich as well? I can't think of one instance when someone told me that they just wanted to be famous without being rich as well. They connected their dream of being well known to a luxurious lifestyle. The truth is, when someone says that they want to be rich and famous, they are really operating on something that they consider nothing more than a dream. In their hearts, they believe that their desire to be rich and famous is okay to ponder, but that it would never apply to them. How do I know that? Simple, I ask them, "Okay, let's get started. You want to be rich and famous, have you taken a specific action or communicated that to any one person? They answer: "No, of course not. When I ask them why? I get answers like:

When I said that I wanted to be rich and famous, it was just a joke.

I don't want to be embarrassed by what other people might think of me.

I really don't believe I have what it takes to be rich and famous.

What if I fail?

It's just a dream, not meant to happen to me.

I really don't know what I want.

There are also those that are in denial.

Of course, I ***will*** tell everyone I know... just not now. I'll do it later.

I just need a little more time to (fill in the blank) first.

I'm going to get it all! All I must do is wish it to be so.

The universe will make it happen for me.

I'm doing it... all of it... but I'll do it tomorrow.

When people say these types of things, you know that they haven't acted on their desire or expressed themselves to anyone at all. Their dream continues to live in the distant future within their imagination and nowhere else. If you don't manifest (act) and say aloud what you want, it will remain in your imagination and will never happen. Why then are people so afraid to announce what they want to the world? This is going to sound strange, but I think it's because they really don't want what they say they want. This has a lot to do with self-doubt and fear of failure. We are all afraid to be criticized, evaluated, and put on the spot. Once you put something out there, people will know it, they will measure it and want to see if what you say you desire will actually happen. Criticism is another major factor. Your friends, family, boyfriends, girlfriends, and spouses will criticize your dream for the simple reason that they may not want to be left behind or they must be envious. However, if your desires are going to become reality, they must be announced to the world orally and in writing. This is step one! You must have the courage to put it out there into the universe in an articulate manner. Why both orally and in writing? Because if you write it down, it has a formality to it. It's written down, for all to see and read. But you may also be hampered by your inability to articulate your desires to the world. This is where an acting class is helpful.

Taking an acting class will help you hone the skills necessary to communicate your dreams and desires to the universe. It's not a "magic bean" like Jack and the Beanstalk but taking an acting class will provide you with the intellectual, emotional, physical, and spiritual tools to communicate and share with others your desires without self-doubt and fear of rejection. But you're thinking: "I'm not yet an actor! I'm just getting started or I don't want to be an actor." The truth is, that you are already acting every day of your life by playing a multitude of characters within the many universes you live in. At home, you're the husband, the wife, the dad, the mom, then at work, the manager, the friend, or the boss. The combinations are endless, and you move from one universe to another every day, and you play them all. The only difference between the actor on stage or screen and you are actors have been trained to play characters for an audience. Actors use their performing skills to communicate a character's intellectual ideas, emotion, physicality, and spirit within the specific universe of a play or film. You can do the same thing within ***your*** real-life universe by learning the same skills and connecting them to your individual personality. By enrolling in an acting class, you can learn the "art of eloquence" and the ability to share your desires to others more effectively. You'll also become a master at communication of ideas, and what you want within a given situation by incorporating these skills into your own life. Understanding the fundamentals of the art of eloquence will change your life for the better. Manifesting your desires is often as simple as communicating those desires to others and asking for their support. This is the core of learning the art of eloquence. Bottom-line, become the "new Sophist" and become proficient at asking for and obtaining what you want out of your life. What's wrong with that?

“

In acting class, teachers talk about how the 'givens' of a situation help define a character.

“

Hill Harper

CHAPTER 4
Taking an Acting Class

Okay, you've decided to take an acting class. What's your next step? Keep in mind, that your first class should be on an introductory level unless you have studied acting previously. Should you enroll in a school program, take an individual class or one-time professional workshop? This depends upon where you live. In larger cities like Los Angeles, Dallas, Chicago, and New York City you will have a multitude of choices of acting classes and programs ranging in cost from $400 a month to over $30,000 per year at conservatory schools. Several of these schools can offer degrees or certificates and will list on their websites what it will cost their current faculty and students who have studied with them who have achieved success. Also, well-known schools, are excellent places to learn the craft of acting, while some are a waste of time and money. Often conservatory schools offer specific tracts and may have a narrow focus on a specific style or aspect of acting. Other schools may center their studies around classical theatre, method acting or comedy and may be too specific or craft-oriented to work for your purposes. So, what's the best type of acting class for you? If you are not going to be a professional actor, you don't need to enroll in a prestigious university or conservatory. A better and less expensive choice would be to consider a community college, university extension program or local theatre.

These classes are more general in approach and will cover fundamental skills and a variety of acting styles. The pros of community college or university extension classes are they are more affordable and are often offered as a series of 4-6 meetings, a weekend intensive or once a week for seventeen weeks. Most models usually culminate in a presentation or show, allowing students to invite outside guests to attend. Having a presentation at the end, will give you the opportunity to get on your feet and perform in front of a live audience. The cons of a community college or extension classes is they often can be very large, and students are accepted on a first come, first-served basis without consideration of academic integrity or talent. When you have a class that is composed of more slackers than committed students, it could bring the overall energy down. If you decide to take a class at a community college, see if you can register as an audit to avoid having to worry about getting credit or grades. Audits usually have full access to the campus and classes without the responsibility of worrying about academic grade requirements like written papers or tests. Many of these classes are now offered online using interactive software such as Zoom.

Individual acting classes taught by acting coaches are another choice. Coaches should have some professional or educational experience in acting. Class sizes are often smaller and contain students focused on specific techniques or acting styles. However, acting classes taught by an acting coach can be hit or miss and I strongly suggest that you check them out on the internet on sites such as Yelp before you commit to any payment. You can search for them within your locality under acting classes, performing arts or specialty schools. Check out the student reviews to get an idea of what is covered and whether students generally recommend the classes. Don't worry if there are a few bad reviews. There will always be individuals who are not going to like classes and post poor reviews. What you should look for is the overall evaluation. If the reviews are generally good, then you should investigate further. Once you narrow your search, you can check out the coach's website, email, or phone directly for class meeting times and cost. A good way to see if the class is right for you is to ask whether you can audit one class for free. This is a common practice, with private classes, whereby the coach of a class will let you sit in and observe during one session. Most of the time, to audit means to watch, not participate in the class. However, don't be discouraged by this because this is a great way for you to experience first-hand what goes on in the class and what type of students attend. You will want a class that is "general" in focus and has a good mix of students with some experience and those that are just starting. The mix of the class is important because acting students learn from one another when doing assignments, exercises and watching others perform.

Another option is taking a class offered by a local theatre company. There are various types of theatre companies across the country. Many are local producers of live theatre with a specific artistic point of view, such as classical, experimental, or musical theatre. Often there is an artistic director and a company of actors, while other venues might be a community theatre with no specific membership. The difference between them may be that a local theatre company may present a preselected season of plays featuring their company members. A local theatre set-up like this might require you to join their company and pay monthly dues as a requirement. As a company member, the class may be available to you for free. Also, as a company member you may be required to perform production duties which may include backstage work, painting sets, being an usher, or running box office during their productions. You would also have the option of acting (if cast) in the plays that are produced. Being a member of a theatre company can be a very rewarding experience but remember ***why*** you are taking an acting class in the first place. If you spend countless hours painting sets, doing make-up or box office in exchange for an acting class, while it may be fun, it might not be the right choice for you. Remember to stay on target and learn skills that are focused on your success and acting career. Better to pay for a class, accomplish what you need, and move forward.

Acting classes are also offered as adult or community programming by local municipalities or parks and recreation departments. I would stay away from these types of classes because they are often offered as a recreational activity rather than a learning experience. What's the difference? Recreational classes are just that... an activity which is designed to provide relaxation and fun. Now I'm okay having fun, but recreational classes are less structured and are generally operated more like a community sport or leisure activity than a class. While you may have lots of fun, there will be little else. You will be better served by an acting class that provides general instruction, in a structured environment where you will have ample opportunities to get up on your feet and perform. The best way to learn and get better at something is to do it as much as you can.

What about online acting classes. With the onset of COVID and indoor restrictions, many students seek acting classes that are offered online. Enrolling in an online class has no geographic limitations. While there is a worthwhile level of interaction and content in such classes, the online format really defeats the purpose of establishing yourself in a group setting and learning from others. This is not to say that a class cannot be offered through Zoom or one of the other online programs where you can have an online group individual and group interaction, but I really think the best method of study would be accomplished in a face-to-face class.

What kinds of classes then should you look for so that you can acquire the skills that will enable you to start acting and get anything you want? You need a serious acting class, but what kind? I'm going to describe several kinds of classes you can take as a beginner. They are in no specific order but rather represent the type of classes you might encounter. I will detail a few of the online options you may want to explore later.

Improvisation Classes: Improvisation or *improv* is a form of live theater which allows actors using their imagination to create the who, what, when, where, and why on the spot. The creation of a plot, characters and dialog of a game or scene are made up in the moment and can be based upon an audience or teacher suggestion. These suggestions can be a scenario (scene idea), a single word, a line, or a "what if?" That serve as a starting point for a scene or game. Improvisation classes are a great way to get started, without the worry of having to memorize dialog and blocking. Blocking refers to specific movements and places your character must be on stage when you perform in a play or scene. When you improvise, you create the who, what, when and where on the spot. This can be terrifying to many people, but it's very "freeing" once you begin to feel comfortable on stage. Improvisation will teach you how to trust your choices and feel more confident. However, there's a syndrome that many students of improvisation classes fall into. It is what I call the "comedy trap."

Many improvisation classes are often structured around the creation of scenarios and characters that lead to comic situations. While comedy is not a bad thing and may seem to be fun, it can often become a barrier to student participation. Invariably, there are some students that are naturally funnier than others. They may have more experience or just be very outrageous and a comic talent. These students have an inert ability to instantly come up with funny one liners or humorous choices on the spot which makes the class laugh. Once this happens, the students who have little experience or are not naturally funny, fall back and watch the naturally comic person create an atmosphere where it is expected that all that is said and done in the class ***must*** be funny. Some teachers encourage this type of behavior from these students, which creates a competitive "topping" syndrome where students attempt to comically top the already comic character or scene. The result is a series of meaningless series of unconnected comic bits. Now if you want to learn to be funny or to build your comic skills, this may be the class for you. But remember, you have got to jump in and be funny or get left behind. Many students who don't have a funny bone, hang back because they believe they cannot compete within the comedy rollercoaster. Their insecurity from their belief that they are not funny prohibits them from ever jumping in and fully participating. Instead, they become permanent spectators who hang back rather than players as the comic rollercoaster moves forward. If the class is a comedy class, then this is to be expected unless you abandon your insecurities and go for the funny yourself. If it is just an improvisation class, focused on acting in general, the situations created on the spot should include both elements of drama and comedy. Remember, even what is funny to an audience, might not be humorous to a character within a given scene. If you choose to take an improvisation class, make sure that the class contains both dramatic and comic elements of improvising. Unfortunately, not all life is funny and for your purposes you should be able to improvise within both dramatic and comic moments. You don't want to be the "clown" of your career or professional environment. What you do want is for your colleagues to trust in your abilities to be both funny and dramatic.

There are many styles and approaches to improvisation that you may encounter. Some focus on the creation of a scene or scenario. A scenario, is a particular situation or event such as:

- Visit the Dentist
- Boarding a bus
- First day in a new job
- Taking a pet to the vets
- Buying contraceptives

- Visiting the Doctor
- Buying a second-hand car
- Having a photo taken
- Choosing a gift for a partner
- Wine tasting
- Visiting someone in hospital
- Firing someone
- Job interview
- Ordering a Wedding Cake
- On a spying mission
- The first men in space
- Visiting parents-in-law
- Getting a signature
- Hypochondriac at the doctors
- Slow service in a restaurant
- Police officer pulls someone over

These examples might be humorous or serious or both. Other types of improvisation classes focus on character development. You will create specific characters which can be based on any number of criteria including your own life experience, a photograph, a news story, a well-known person, made up word or idea. For your purposes as a beginning actor, character-based improvisation will be a better fit. The characters and situations you create for them should be real to you, so you can use that character to focus on the circumstances that are created. You can rely on what you do every day of your life, so that you can become proficient at being able to communicate effectively, be a better actor and get what you want.

Where to study improvisation depends upon the city or town that you live in. You can find improvisation classes at your local community college or theater groups. If you live in a city such as Los Angeles or New York, there are many including the Groundlings, Second City or Upright Citizens Brigade (UCB). I have included a few examples located in Los Angeles. You will want to check for similar organizations in your community that offer improvisation classes. Again, make sure you check them out before enrolling to make sure what they are doing fits your needs. For example, UCB is more focused on comedy than just straight improvisation. However, their work, while it is funny, contains both elements of drama and comedy.

GROUNDLINGS IMPROV – CLASSES FOR BEGINNERS

https://groundlings.com/school/online-classes

These classes are great for actors and beginning actors interested in exploring the concepts of improvisation in a fun and welcoming environment. The class is designed to build self-confidence and creativity. No audition is required. There are six three-hour classes in each session.

SECOND CITY – HOLLYWOOD, CALIFORNIA –

https://www.secondcity.com/courses/hollywood/adult/

The Improvisation Program is a complete foundation in the principles of scenic improvisation as practiced at The Second City. Based on the work of Viola Spolin, this five-level program covers all elements of the improvisational process. Students begin in Level A with ensemble, continuing with environment and object work, and end in Level E by rehearsing and performing a fully improvised show.

UPRIGHT CITIZENS BRIGADE (UCB) – Los Angeles

https://losangeles.ucbtrainingcenter.com

The Upright Citizens Brigade Improvisational and Sketch Comedy Training Center is the only accredited improvisational and sketch comedy school in the country. Their faculty represents the best writers and performers working in comedy today. Over the last 15 years, the Upright Citizens Brigade (Matt Besser, Amy Poehler, Ian Roberts, and Matt Walsh) have developed a unique unified curriculum that is constantly updated and improved. With facilities in New York and Los Angeles, the UCB Training Centers offer comedy courses seven days a week at convenient times and locations. In cooperation with the Upright Citizens Brigade, theater students have a chance to perform and learn from current alumni in a popular venue. UCB Training Center teachers and alumni include writers and performers from *Saturday Night* Live, The *Tonight Show*, Key *&* *Peele*, *Silicon Valley*, *Veep*, The *Daily Show, Inside Amy Schumer*, *Master of None*, *Drunk History*, *Full Frontal with Samantha Bee* and many other hit television shows and movies. Check their website for current offerings and prices

With improv, it's a combination
of listening and
not trying to be funny.
Kristen Wiig

Scene Study

A scene study class focuses on the actor's role within a set script with multiple characters, dialog, and storyline. Scenes can be part of a larger work (play or screenplay) or stand-alone from a scene book. You will learn how to structure a scene into parts or beats; how to create a character within a particular universe and determine their intentions and obstacles blocking them. When we speak in a certain way or do things in our own lives, these actions are motivated by outcomes that we seek to achieve. A scene offers you an opportunity to create a character with a specific motivation and desire for a certain outcome within the scene. But it's not just about what your character's motivation. You will also encounter obstacles (other characters, things, and situations) which prevent your character from getting what they want. You will have to learn how to overcome obstacles. Don't be concerned if this seems complicated because we do the same thing in life. When you ask your supervisor for a day off, what is happening? You are making a request that you want fulfilled and you conduct yourself in a certain manner designed to achieve the desired outcome. This manner includes the way you speak, the words you choose, and the physicality you assume within that specific situation. This is the same process that happens when a character in a scene interacts with another character. Taking a scene study class will give you lots of practice and you'll become proficient at communicating clearly and getting what you want in your personal and professional life. But now you're wondering, if this is something you will want to learn, how can you get proficient at it? You can acquire these skills in an acting technique class by participating in a variety of scenes, characters, and situations. It's the adage, "practice makes perfect."

An acting technique class can you help you focus on specific acting methods to create realistic characters using both internal and external methods. What exactly is a technique in relation to acting? It is a specific method of achieving a certain reality when developing and performing a character in a play or film. There are acting classes which focus upon a single technique such as what is known as the "method." The method is a technique of acting in which an actor strives to achieve an emotional identification with a character. This system has its roots in the theories of Konstantin Stanislavsky (a director in turn of the century Russia) and was introduced to the United States in the 1930s. Method acting was taught in acting workshops and studios, including the Actors' Studio in New York City under the teaching of Elia Kazan and Lee Strasberg. This form of acting is associated with actors such as Marlon Brando, Dustin Hoffman, and Al Pacino.

There are other classes that teach a variety of internal and external techniques so that an actor has several options to rely upon when creating a character. Other types of technique classes may include the classical studies, Stanislavski, Meisner Technique, Uta Hagen, or Viola Spolin. These methods include a variety of internal and external techniques that can be utilized to create an intellectual, emotional, physical, and spiritual aspect of a character.

I suggest for your purposes as a beginning actor that you try to get into a class that teaches a variety of techniques to give you the most comprehensive exposure to acting. The availability and variety of technique classes will vary by your location. In larger cities like New York City or Los Angeles, there will be an extensive variety of classes to take. If you live in a city with a limited offering of classes, try to find one that has a variety of techniques and remember you can take an online class. What kinds of technique classes might you encounter?

Classical:

A general term for a technique of creating a role and act that focuses on using the expressive elements of the physical body, vocal technique, tradition, imagination, using both external and internal methods to achieve a character's intellectual, emotional, and physical state. Classical acting technique has many sources and can be based upon the theories of period actors and directors including Konstantin Stanislavski, Michel Saint-Denis. Also, this technique can also be traced to the traditions of ancient Greece, Ancient Rome, Shakespeare, Commedia dell'arte, and Romantic melodrama.

Stanislavski:

This realistic acting technique has its roots at the end of the nineteenth and beginning of the twentieth centuries and focuses on an internal approach to the creation and performance of a character within a play or film. This technique was developed as a reaction to the largely artificial acting techniques of the period. The Stanislavski method encourages performers to draw upon their own feelings and personal experiences to convey the "truth" or core of a character they are portraying. The Stanislavski technique refers to this as affective memory, which essentially means that the actor must refer to their past experiences just as a painter would use the specific colors on his/her palette to create a unique one-of-a-kind character. This is a valuable technique for you to learn and experience because it requires you to put yourself in the mindset of the character exploring elements that are in common to yourself to give a more genuine portrayal of the character. When you relate to other individuals in life or business, this is a valuable skill to have.

Method Acting:

This technique is sometimes referred to as the "American" interpretation of the Stanislavski system, but that would define it too narrowly. The "method" is a variety of techniques used as tools for actors to comprehend the totality of relating to and the portrayal of a character within a play or film. The Method was formulated by the famous acting teacher Lee Strasberg. Strasberg's method technique is based upon a simple concept that actors should develop an intellectual, emotional, and physical understanding of their roles by relying upon their own experiences. This is like Stanislavski's affective *memory* but has evolved the technique to include the terms *"emotional memory"* and *"emotional recall" which requires actors* use their recollections of their personal memories to evoke their character's emotions and physicality. The method then is rooted within the foundations found in Stanislavski's technique but other acting techniques are also based on Stanislavski's ideas, such as those of Stella Adler and Sanford Meisner, of but these are not considered "method acting." The method, like Stanislavski's technique, can be a valuable tool to teach you how to interact with others and get what you want in your personal and professional life. What about the Meisner technique?

The Meisner Technique is based upon the idea that acting finds its true meaning and expression using both physicality and emotional approaches to creating a role. It is based upon the Stanislavski system but relies more on the individual moment and your character's reaction to it. It requires the actor to focus totally on the other actor as though they are real, and they only exist in that moment. This is a method that makes the actors in the scene seem more authentic to the audience. If we focus on the reality of the scene from moment to moment, isn't this what we do every day in our own lives?

Acting classes in your community can be offered in a variety of techniques and delivery methods. The important thing to remember, is that you want to focus on learning to be more comfortable when relating to other people and you acquire skills of expression that you can utilize on stage, in front of a camera, your career and everyday life.

Other types of classes

There are other types of classes that focus on specific parts of professional acting that you can learn useful skills as a beginning actor.

Audition Classes (also called Cold Reading classes)

Audition classes focus on the specific skills needed for professional actors to audition for stage and film productions. If you are a beginning actor, you may feel that this type of class will have no value for you. However, I want you to think about what an audition really is? It's a sales pitch. The actor relies upon, skill, appearance, and demeanor to audition to play a character in a play, movie, television show or commercial. Have you ever been in a situation when you were required to convince someone of your way of thinking about an idea? I know the answer is "yes." I don't care if you are a mail carrier, checkout clerk at a grocery store or a person who works in an office setting. This can also apply to your life if you are in a situation when you must persuade individuals to your way of thinking. Persuasive situations happen to all of us every day of our lives. An audition class will help you hone the skills to imagine a character, sell a product, create agreement, and persuade individuals to your way of thinking about a particular idea.

Before we leave this section, I want to let you know what the term "cold reading" refers to in relation to acting. A cold reading is a method of audition used in theatre, film, television, or commercials. It is an audition when an actor reads out loud from one or more pages of a script or other text with little or no rehearsal, practice, or study in advance. The truth about cold readings are that they are rarely cold. Actors usually can download the script pages (sides) in advance and often memorize their lines for the audition. Whether the audition is a cold reading, or a prepared scene remember that is really selling yourself, an idea to a producer or casting director that the actor is perfect for the role. When you express an idea, sell yourself, a character, or product, you are seeking agreement. Remember not all cold readings or auditions will result in a positive outcome. An audition class will teach you how to do that. Here are some examples from Los Angeles:

The Hollywood Acting Workshop

Professional-level television, commercial and film acting classes for adults and teenagers, from beginning to advanced levels. Classes are focused on improving communication skills, self-esteem, and confidence in a supportive environment. They offer four weeks of once-per week workshops. Check their website for current offerings and prices. This is an affordable and ideal starting point to learn about acting and if you want a professional career in acting, how to break into the business. The emphasis of the workshops is scripted scenes, mock auditions, monologues and on camera technique with in-class DVD playback and instructor feedback. Classes are offered online internationally. **http://hollywoodactingworkshop.com**

***Cold Reading: Jamison Haase at* LA On Camera Training Center**

A class in which each actor performs a recorded cold reading, usually with minimal time to prepare. This is good preparation for auditioning. They also cover on camera techniques such as close-ups vs. a wide shot and what an actor can do to maximize those moments. Check their website for current offerings and prices. http://laoncamera.com

On Camera Acting Classes

On camera acting classes can be a combination of scene study, cold readings, audition techniques or monologues which focus on the actor's performance in front of a camera. This is an excellent way to get a sense of how you sound and what you look like on camera and by extension in life. But be careful, you won't look, and sound exactly the way you see yourself on camera. Most classes, film their students using a single camera and a lavalier, overhead or shotgun microphone. A lavalier will be a small microphone that will be clipped onto your clothing; an overhead will be held over the space you are speaking, and a shotgun will be attached to the camera. You will be lit by ambient room light or one or two small spotlights. The result is rather poor sound quality and uneven uncomplimentary lighting. Students see themselves and ask: "Do I really sound and look that bad?" The answer is "no." Remember, a classroom studio will not have perfect lighting or sound, but it can give you a general idea of how you look on camera.

The purpose of a camera class is to familiarize the students with working in front of a camera, not producing a film for distribution. Instead of focusing on the quality of the playback, point, your attention on the intimacy of the camera. The camera can highlight fundamental qualities of your physicality, demeanor, and vocal projection. Taking an on-camera class, can reveal small idiosyncrasies that you may have when you speak or move. A common on is that individuals slap their hands on their legs when they are trying to emphasize something they are saying. This physical action dissipates rather than strengthens how they communicate. Once you see it on camera, you will know what it is and stop doing it. Seeing yourself on camera can give you the kind of feedback that you will not be able to obtain looking into the mirror in the morning. Whether you are doing a cold reading, a scene or improvising an on-camera class will help you get a sense of yourself so that you may see your strengths and correct your weaknesses. Here are some examples.

Carolyne Barry Creative Ent.

The Carolyne Barry studio prides itself on teaching actors to offer something that casting directors must have. The studio's classes are meant to teach actors how to develop an on-camera persona. Other aspects of the program include commercial monologues, interviewing, and product handling. The studio also offers a hosting workshop, which lets students explore a broad view of hosting roles and teleprompter training. Some workshops feature a one-night lesson from commercial casting directors and commercial directors. Many are available using Zoom. Check their website for individual class costs carolynbarry.com

Commercial Acting Classes

Commercial Acting classes or workshops focus on auditioning for and performing in commercials for television, live presentation, or social media. You will learn how use performance space, create moments; you will get a sense of yourself as you relate to specific scenarios. Almost all commercial acting workshops are on camera. You will have to present yourself in a very specific way within a specific time frame. What makes commercial acting different than film, television or theatre the casting process focuses on your look, physicality, and demeanor. You may have to improvise within a given framework or work with specific lines or actions. Remember, you are selling a product, service, or idea and you should find personal traits within yourself that connect with the idea and content presented in each commercial spot. You will learn branding skills that will give you the ability to "brand" yourself within a given universe. Commercial acting skills will make you proficient at conceptualizing ideas you want to promote in your own life and career. Here are some examples of commercial classes:

Terry Berland's six-week commercial acting workshop

Terry Berland's Six Week Commercial Acting Workshop utilizes a unique technique based on the same solid elements it takes to make an actor's audition stand out in a film or television short scene. This commercial technique workshop covers building a strong foundational base to support acting choices which lead to a textured performance that appears realistic, simple, and seamless. Participants will be able to create a performance in 30 seconds that is specific and will stand out. This workshop is designed to free you from any inhibitions you may have, to make what you do enjoyable, to trust yourself, gain self- confidence, and enable you to create fully within the small time and space you are given to audition. http://www.berlandcasting.com/oc/

Commercial and voice acting workshops tend to be more expensive for classes with multiple sessions and where there is recording involved. There are lower cost alternatives such as community college extension or adult education classes. Community colleges might cost an average of $50 for a series of not-for credit classes. But most colleges lack the appropriate equipment to record your work and tend to have larger classes. So, you won't get to perform in front of a camera as much as you would in a private class. Another alternative is a one-day workshop which can last anywhere from two to four hours. These workshops are usually, taught by working professionals, casting directors or agents and have a limited enrollment. You will be able to get up several times and have your reading or presentation critiqued on the spot. A great way to find these shorter classes is through a website called Course Horse

https://coursehorse.com/nyc/classes/performing-arts/acting.

Classes are divided by city and subject. Average cost: Free to $20 to $199, depending upon the class length and number of students. Most of the classes are in the $20-$50 range.

Vocal and Voice Over Classes

Vocal and Voice Over: The proper use of your voice in any professional setting is important. A vocal class will improve the quality of your voice, projection, or resonance. A voice over class, will cover many of the same components that you might learn in a vocal class. However, a voice over class primarily will focus on your voice, diction and tone as those voice qualities relate to working professionally as a voice actor. You will work on commercials, narration, documentary, e-learning, corporate industrials and creating character voices for animation. Also, most voice over classes provide a demo disk of your voice assignments completed as part of the class. I will discuss these types of classes separately. First, vocal classes.

Vocal classes will teach you how to master vocal quality and diction. You will learn how to use your voice to the best of its ability including how to breath properly and how to control it. Remember, these classes are not to develop your singing voice. The goal of a vocal class is to learn how to be more aware of your speaking abilities, which are essential to master if you want to communicate effectively. Average cost: $50 - $75 for 60 minutes for a one-on-one session. If you are part of a larger class, as little as $100 for 5 to 7 weekly sessions.

Voice Over classes aren't the same as vocal classes but can help you develop some of the same types of skills. A voice-over acting class will help you master all the technical skills you need to have to become a voice-over actor and work professionally. You will also learn how to breathe, improve your vocal quality, and diction. This type of class can be valuable for you if you approach it as an addition to stage and film techniques. Average cost: $450 to $550 for 5 to 7 weekly sessions including a VO Demo Disk or thumb drive at the conclusion. You can investigate VOCAL and VOICE OVER courses at Course Horse.

https://coursehorse.com/los-angeles/classes/performing-arts/acting/more-acting/vocal

These are good for a beginning actor with an average cost: Under $100 total for one to three sessions.

Body and Movement Classes

Your physicality is just as important as your vocal quality as a actor and when communicating with individuals or groups of people. If you appear uncomfortable and closed, anyone you interact with will absorb that same energy. You want to appear balanced, confident, with clarity and strength when you are communicating your ideas. You will explore the physicality of every part of your body as it relates to the given space you occupy and how your appearance and actions relate to others. What kinds of classes can you take? Some classes may be described in terms of dance and may not be described as "body and movement" What you should be looking for at the beginning is more movement and less dance. The difference is movement is how your body reacts to the space it occupies. Dance, on the other hand, is more formal and may be tied to a specific technique such as ballet, modern, hip-hop or modern. You may also achieve a better connection with your physicality by taking a yoga class. The goal is to be more connected to your physicality and understand how your movement through space can influence your ability to communicate to others. Approximate Cost: $20 for a movement class.

There are many different types of acting classes. The most important thing for you to remember is that you want to improve your ability to communicate intellectually, emotionally, physically, and spiritually on stage, in front of a camera. You can also use these same skills in your private life. You can pick one or more of these class types to focus on what you need to work on. Remember, everything takes some time; don't be afraid to spend a few months to a year in one class and then move on to something else to continue improving. One last item about taking classes is the teacher.

Your teacher

Remember, not every acting teacher will be a perfect fit for each student. Teachers all have different styles of teaching and areas of acting that they feel are important. You must find teachers that are a good fit for you. A good fit means that they fulfill the goals you are trying to achieve and provide constructive criticism. That means when you perform, they build upon your strengths rather than tear you down. Look for a teacher that will encourage you and not berate or severely criticize you if you don't do exactly what they expect. There are some teachers who regard themselves as super gurus and harshly criticize anyone who doesn't do exactly what they say. Stay away from this type of teacher and find one that will tell you what you did correctly and what you need to work on. Tell them that you are taking an acting class as a beginner, and you want to work on getting started. You still must do the same work as everyone else in the class, but by creating a personal framework around you will help your teacher focus on what you need to accomplish. Now let's look at your first day of school!

“

In acting class, they tell you that you must be real, connect with the people, connect with your partner. The same as politics, you must connect to the people.

“

Arnold Schwarzenegger

CHAPTER 5
Your First Day of Acting Class

How to Say Hello

A performing arts student should take an acting class to develop their performance skills, for stage or film performance. However, assume that whatever class you enroll that it will only be populated by actors wanting to improve their skills. There are an infinite number of reasons people sign up for an acting class. If it's a college, they may want a course they believe will be an easy "A." Others take an acting class to meet new people and make friends. You are taking an acting class to get started and connect to the skills to be successful in your acting career, personal and professional life. It is important when you introduce yourself to a new group of people to let them know a little bit about yourself and create a position of yourself that fits the goal you are trying to achieve.

What is a position?

Positioning is a marketing concept that outlines what a business should do to market its product or service to its customers. In positioning, the marketing department creates an image for the product based on its intended audience. This is created using promotion, price, place, and product.

Lynn Lauren, Lynn (2019, February 1st) - What Is Positioning in a Marketing Plan? - https://smallbusiness.chron.com/positioning-marketing-plan-22983.html

The same protocol exists for your acting class, that you should develop at your job. You should create a specific "position" describing who you are in the minds of anyone you meet. Remember, positioning in advertising refers to a significant place that a brand occupies in the mind of the consumer and how it is distinguished from other products from its competitors. In your scenario, you are the product or brand and like an advertiser you should emphasize the distinguishing features you may possess and create an image or position in everyone's mind about you. Once your position within a group has been achieved, it can become difficult to change it. How you first introduce yourself to a new group is very important. You must create a position for yourself. But you must choose wisely and remember that an acting class by its very nature is working with other individuals in the class. Sometimes, your acting class teacher will do this for you by asking you to introduce yourself to the class.

When I begin an acting class, I start by asking each new student to stand up in front of the entire group and answer three simple questions.

1. State your name: I ask them to tell the group their name that they prefer to be called rather than their legal name that might appear on a class roster. This is always an interesting process because the name that they prefer to be called often has no resemblance to their actual name. They might rattle off a long multi-part name like Louis George Maurice Delgado III and then quickly add, but you can call me "Lucky." The name that they prefer to be called is often the key to **who they really are, what they want out of their lives and how they wish to be perceived by others.** Next question.

2. Why are you taking this class? – You're thinking this is really easy "to learn how to act." But that's often not the answer you get. It's always interesting, at least to me, why a person decides to take an acting class in the first place. The reasons I have heard in some of my college-level classes range from **"I'm looking for an easy A," "I'd like to give acting a try," "This is the only class that works for my schedule"** or simply "I don't know I thought it might be fun." I want to hold on to that last idea that an acting class sounds like it might be fun. The truth is for many of those people who think it might be fun, it turns out to be quite the opposite. Taking an acting class forces many to face the many insecurities they may have about themselves, their physical appearance, and their fear of being on a stage in front of others. We will talk more about this later. Now on to the third question that gets to the core of who these people are. Now, the third question.

3. Tell us something interesting about yourself that we can remember you by:

Remember, each new student walks to the center of the stage and introduces themselves to a group of people they have never met before. They are a blank page in the eyes of their new classmates and can frame themselves in any way they want. Here are some examples.

FRED SMITH

Hello, my name is Frederick Smith, most people call me Fred. I have always been interested in taking an acting class even though I have never done acting before. I am usually very nervous when I get up in front of people and I wanted to work on that. Something interesting about me that you might be able to remember is that I'm a marathon runner. Thank you.

Once that introduction is made, the class usually applauds while Fred walks back to his seat and sits down. Then, the next person walks to the center of the stage. But something else is a play here. Fred has made a connection with the new group classmates that operates on three distinct levels: intellectual, emotional, and physical. Once that connection is established, the audience will have a certain impression or position in their minds about Fred that will last until it is changed either by Fred himself or by external circumstances. The next time a member of the class meets Fred, they may not remember his name, but they more than likely will remember what he does. They will say to themselves, "he's the marathon guy." Now let's stop for a moment. If you conjure up images of a person who is known as the "marathon guy," what adjectives might you attach to them?

Physically fit

Disciplined

Competitive

Healthy

Fast

A leader

A winner

Fred has made a connection with the group which will remain until it is replaced by another connection. He's the ***marathon guy***. Later, Fred might do something memorable in class like a dramatic or comedic scene. That event will then replace or add to the "marathon guy" connection established in his introduction with "There's Fred, he's the marathon runner but more so he's a really good actor that did that dramatic monologue in class last week." This series of connections and disconnections will continue if Fred remains part of the group. One could argue that our fictional student Fred had little or no control over his relationship and position within the class. The driving factor that established Fred's relationship was at first that he was a "marathon runner," and then secondly that he was a "good actor." However, the only time Fred really had full control of his relationship within that universe of the class was on the first day, of the first class and the first time he said hello. At that moment, Fred controlled all aspects of the message. Any resulting image that the class develops concerning Fred would be based upon his subsequent actions and circumstances his involved with. Those later elements are based on an already established position within the group and are not under his control. What if Fred were a lousy actor, could he still function within the group and be successful? The answer is "yes." If he were not a great actor but still held the position of marathon runner, he would be simply that. "Fred the marathon runner that needs to work on his acting. What occurs is sense of group agreement of what Fred's position is within the universe of the acting class. This is called "creation of agreement." Someone once said to me, "What makes a star a star?" Answer: "Agreement." If we all agree that this person is a star within their universe, then they are a star or the "can do" person," or "the marathon runner,"or the person to stay away from. The position is created at the first introduction. Once the position is set, the process reinvention begins. However, remember one thing, the first position created is the most difficult to change once it is established. This is not to say that it can't be changed. It is just more difficult. In the case of our student Fred, he may evolve from the "marathon runner, to the best actor in the class. But he will still be thought of as the "marathon guy who is the best actor in the class." These connections exist for famous people as well. I am thinking of Monica Lewinsky, who is well past her affair with former president Bill Clinton. However, no matter what she does now or in the future, she will always be connected to her affair with Clinton. This was the first impression that defines any future addition.

Let's look at another example of a first-time class introduction. This next student named Sally is a new member of a class and like Fred she has been asked to introduce herself, say a few words about why she decided to take the class and lastly something interesting that we can all remember her by.

SALLY

Why I took this class. I've always thought it would be interesting to try to be something you're not. Something interesting about me is that… well I really don't have anything interesting to say about myself. I guess I'm just kind of ordinary … just like everybody else here. Thank you.

Before anyone can applaud, Sally makes a quick exit to her seat. First, Sally has forgotten to introduce herself to the class. She hasn't said her name, which makes it difficult for anyone sitting in the room, to make a connection to her. She also has identified herself as uninteresting and then in the same breath connected the idea of being uninteresting to the rest of the group. Her introduction sounds something like this. ***"Hi, I'm not telling you my name because I am uninteresting and boring just like you. I am unworthy of any notice or recognition."*** Sally has created the perfect scenario that will guarantee she will be forgotten moments after she has taken her seat. To quote a line from the motion picture Austin Powers *"…throw me a frickin bone here."* You must give the group something tangible to work with. Saying you are uninteresting and by extension unworthy of comment, will get you nothing. As Sally may never really become part of the universe of that group setting because she has set herself up as a standalone unworthy of being included, and if she were included it would somehow imply that the group was just as uninteresting as she was. Can Sally still function within the group and be successful? Answer "yes" but after her initial introduction, with great difficulty. Once your uninteresting position within a group setting has been established, who would want to work with her? Just thinking about working with her would be an automatic "you are uninteresting too" badge that you would have to wear. Collectively, you might be positioned as the "losers" in the group. A group image difficult to change once established. What is the answer?

When you introduce yourself in a group setting you must frame yourself within the ideal. I don't want you to lie or just say impossibly nice things about yourself. You can just focus more on your strengths and then frame your weaknesses as something you are working on. Create the person that you aspire to be citing your achievements rather than boxing yourself into your failures, highlighting what you didn't achieve. It doesn't matter if you are totally where you want to be. What's more important is that you don't limit yourself by a negative self-view. How would Sally improve her introduction?

SALLY JONES

Hello, my name is Sally Jones. I am a veterinary assistant. I love animals and love being able to go to a job everyday where I can help them. I'm taking this class, because

I have always been a bit shy and wanted to work on becoming more comfortable when connecting with people.

(Beat)

Something you don't know about me is that I am a volunteer at an animal rescue on the weekends. I help animals (mostly dogs and cats) that have been abandoned or abused. I am very excited to be in this class and look forward to getting to know each one of you. Thank you.

What's Sally's position now? "The kind but quiet animal lover." Someone nice that you would like to get to know. What adjectives describe Sally?

Kind

Nice person

Animal lover

Compassionate

Hard working

Loving

Shy

Dedicated

Giving

Sally, by focusing on the positive rather than negative, has created an entirely different position of herself within the universe of the class. She didn't mention acting, but that didn't matter because the qualities that would be used to describe her, also work within the framework of an actor in a class. Wouldn't you want to work with an actor that was hard-working, dedicated, giving and kind? What would Sally's position be? "Hard working animal lover" or "Shy, but hard-working animal lover." What about the shy part? The fact that Sally is shy is not a total negative. Most people are a bit or a lot shy when they first meet new people. I think almost anyone getting up in front of a group of people for the first time is shy. She also said that she was taking the class to work on her shyness… what's not to like?

You may wonder, why would Sally or any other person present themselves in a such a demeaning way? It's important to think our real thought bubble when we present ourselves for the first time to anyone. You say hello, then immediately visualize what the group or person is thinking about you. Your thought bubble might be:

What do they really think of me?

I'm so fat.

The clothes I'm wearing look like rags.

They are all so smart and I'm not

I'd rather be home watching TV.

None of these people like me.

I hate my body.

I hate my hair

I hate my teeth

I smell bad

I have absolutely no luck

Everyone gets all the lucky breaks, but not me.

These people make more money than I do

These people are successful and I'm not

I'm a loser

The real question is why do we project these negative thoughts about ourselves? This may sound absurd, but we think and project these thoughts to provide comfort. Once we've established ourselves at a lower value, we don't have to worry about criticism or challenge because we have removed them. Once you've established yourself as inadequate, you're done. You can sit back and relax and let the world go by. The problem is, if you put yourself at the bottom, that's probably where you will remain. While we all admire redemption, it is very difficult to change the initial position that someone creates when we first meet them.

I want you to make a list of positive adjectives that truly describe you and that you could weave into an introduction. If it is hard for you to come up with a list of at least five, ask friends, family, and people you work with. Also, you can look up examples on the internet of traits that would accurately describe you:

http://ideonomy.mit.edu/essays/traits.html

Here are a few examples: adaptable, calm, caring, considerate, disciplined. energetic, fair, fun loving, courteous, hardworking, helpful, honest, or imaginative. I suggest you look up the full list and try to come up with at least five positive traits that would describe you for the first time to a larger group or individual. Try to be honest, don't say things about yourself that plainly aren't true. If you start with a lie, you will have to keep it up every time you see this group of people.

There was a producer that I met who had a habit of rattling off the names of celebrities that he said he knew personally. He often mentioned Robert DeNiro like they were best friends and called him "Bobby." One night at dinner in Malibu, California, this producer was bragging about what he said and did with "Bobby" when Robert DeNiro walked into the same restaurant. I said, what luck, there's Bobby! He turned to see Robert DeNiro and sank down as low as he could almost under the table. It was obvious that he had never met Robert DeNiro and likely any of the celebrities he said he knew. The lesson here, don't make outrageous things up about yourself that force you to live a lie. Once you head down that path, the universe will catch up with you sooner or later. Better to be yourself and the universe will do the rest.

PHYSICALITY

Now that we have discussed what you will say in your introduction, let's talk about how you will present yourself physically. If you are not used to getting up in front of people, you are going to be nervous. You won't know what to do with your hands; you might shuffle, have a racing pulse, cracking voice or feel nauseous. What creates these conditions when we stand up in front of a group to introduce ourselves? First, you want your introduction to be perfect in every way so you will be accepted and liked. You raise the stakes and want every physical movement you do to reflect this flawless person. However, here's the trap; nothing is perfect, so you set yourself up for imperfection and failure. But before you do this, I want you to know the following.

A. **Nobody cares.**

I don't want you to think I'm mean. But everyone else in the room is focused on their own turn and what they will say or have said.

B. If you make a mistake, use it:

Make everything you do part of your introduction. If you forget something because you are nervous, use it. If you stumble, then make it part of your introduction. If you forget your name (this happens) ask for help. In short, make everything you do (even the mistakes) part of the introduction.

C. You don't have to be funny:

You don't have to think of humorous things to say to make people interested in you. Instead, think about sharing something that is interesting and true about yourself.

D. There is nothing that you can do or say that is wrong:

Of course, if you are rude to your audience or say inappropriate things, those would be bad choices. What I am referring to is your set plan of what you will say or do if it goes off course. Just go with it.

E. Acknowledge that you are nervous:

If you are nervous (and everybody is nervous no matter what they say), what do you do? Acknowledge it by simply saying that you don't do this often or have never done it and that you are nervous. As soon as you acknowledge that you are nervous, most of that type of tension will go away for both you and your audience.

F. Take your time:

You don't have to talk in slow motion, but you should share an idea and give your audience the opportunity to take that in and react. Think of a game of tennis. One player hits the ball over the net and then a second player reacts to it and then hits it back. Think in terms of a back and forth between you and your audience rather than rapidly rattling out a list of things you want to say about yourself and running back to your chair.

Now that you have those ideas under your belt, what about physicality? What do you do with your hands and how do you stop shaking? I don't want to sound like your mother, but I want you to put your shoulders back, don't slouch, and move deliberately with purpose. Moving deliberately means however you move within a space, be definite about it. Don't start one movement and then drop it for another. This type of incomplete physicality makes you look unsure, untruthful, and uninteresting. When you make a movement complete it. Even if it turns out to be wrong for you at that moment, complete it and make it part of what you planned to do.

If you feel like you won't be able at first to stand up in an open space, you can put your foot up on a stool or other object. This will help you channel the nervous energy into a solid object and will ground you. But this is a crutch you should lose very quickly once you get more comfortable in front of other people. If you are grounded by an object, remember to use that object for that purpose only. Don't focus your comments downward toward it. Remember, you are introducing yourself for the first time and want people to know something about who you are. Now you are in the class, what happens next?

“

Acting is all about honesty. If you can fake that, you've got it made.

“

George Burns

CHAPTER 6

Acting Class Terminology
What to Know to Succeed

Acting class terminology:

The following list of terms is not all inclusive but represents generally most of the terminology you will encounter in a face to face or online acting class. I have included some film terms if you are enrolled in a on camera acting class. I think the purpose of becoming familiar with these terms will allow you to function freely within the class environment even though you may be learning these skills for a non-acting reason rather than an acting career.

Terms for Acting on the Stage:

PRESENTATIONAL

When the reality of the audience is the same as the performer. The performer acknowledges and interacts with the audience. Example: Stand Up Comedy, asides.

REPRESENTATIONAL

When the reality of the audience is different than character or performer. The performer does not acknowledge or interact with the audience. Example: Chekhov, Miller, Ibsen.

PARA THEATRICAL

Having some qualities of live Theatre but not all. Examples include mimes, jugglers, street performers, and magicians.

DIRECTOR

The person, who provides the point of view for the presentation of the play and directs

the action.

STAGE MANAGER

The person in charge of all elements of a play during the run of a performance.

PLAYWRIGHT

A person who writes (DESCRIPTION, ACTION, DIALOGUE) in the form of a play to be presented orally or on stage.

DESIGNERS

The people who create the "universe" of the play including sound, lighting, costume, setting, props and special effects.

DRESS / TECHNICAL REHEARSAL

A full rehearsal with complete technical accompaniment during the final production phase before opening.

STAGING TYPES:

PROSCENIUM:

The performer "P" is on one side and the audience 'A" is on another. Ideal for plays which require extensive sets and back drops.

THRUST

The performer "P" has the audience "A" on three sides. There is some limitation to the kinds of sets that can be used because of sight lines. There is increased audience interaction. Example:

ARENA OR ROUND

The performer "P" has the audience "A" on all four sides. Ideal intimacy with the audience, however there are limitations as to what kind of set can be used because of sight lines. Increased audience reaction.

ENVIRONMENTAL

The audience area and the performing are one. The audience and the performer share the same space. Increased opportunity for interaction and intimacy. Example: Toni and Tina's Wedding and Tamara.

FLIES:

The area above the stage in which set piece and flats are suspended.

WINGS

The area to either side of the stage in which set pieces, props, lights, and flats can be stored. Also, an area for actors to position themselves before entering a scene.

UPSTAGE

The direction away from the audience in a proscenium Theatre.

DOWNSTAGE

The direction toward the audience in a proscenium Theatre.

STAGE RIGHT /LEFT

The actor's right and left when facing the audience in a proscenium Theatre.

HOUSE

The area in a theatre/auditorium where the audience sits.

MOVEMENT ON THE STAGE

BLOCKING

The actor's movement upon the stage When an actor obstructs the view of an actor or action on the stage

CROSS

Movement of an actor from one end of the stage or area to another.

CHEATING

When an actor is opens the action so that the audience may see the action more clearly.

STAGE BUSINESS

Small actions performed by an actor which may enhance character or develop plot.

UPSTAGING

When an actor does business behind another actor or places their body behind another actor forcing the audience or the actor to look the upstage activity.

An act or action which takes place behind the main action. This draws the audience attention away from what it should be looking at.

PANTOMIME

Performing without words, expressing meaning through physical actions/gestures.

CHARACTER CREATION - PERFORMANCE TERMS

CHARACTERIZATION

The process of creating a character whose words and actions are determined by the elements of the play.

AD-LIB

Speech or action that is done by the actor within the context of the scene that has not been specifically written or rehearsed.

IMPROVISATION

Actor creates the scene in its entirety. Creation of who, what, when and where.

SUBTEXT

The underlying meaning to the scene not always apparent in the dialogue.

MOTIVATION

The character's reason for doing what he/she does within a moment, scene, act, or entire play.

INTNENTION

What the character wants from the other character(s) in a scene

PICKING UP CUES

When an actor is asked to shorten the time between when a cue is given and his/her response.

STAGE WHISPER

A whisper that is not supposed to be heard by the audience.

DICTION

The actor's ability to be understood.

FOURTH WALL

An imaginary wall between the actors and the audience.

PRIMARY CHARACTER

The character that the story is about. "Macbeth" in the play Macbeth

SECONDARY CHARACTER

The Character that serves the story line. Provides information and action. For example, a messenger, butler, or confidant.

MONOLOGUE

One character speaking his/her lines either to themselves, another character, or the audience.

SOLILOQUY

A monologue that represents the inner workings of a character's mind.

TOPPING A LINE

An actor responding to a line with more volume or intensity than the line before them.

BEAT

A pause of varying length during a scene that is being played out. This beat is usually taken to emphasize emotion or thought or action.

TYPES OF PROPS

SET PROPS

Those props that belong to a particular set piece (not a character) Example would be a library book that might be on a library set.

COSTUME PROP

A prop that belongs to a specific costume such as a whip with a riding costume.

CHARACTER PROP

A prop that belongs to a particular character such as Sherlock Holmes' pipe.

STAGE PROP

Any prop that belongs to a specific set. For example, if a scene took place in an antique shop, the antiques would be the stage props.

CHARACTER CREATION - PERFORMANCE TERMS

PRESENTATIONAL

When the reality of the audience is the same as the performer. The performer acknowledges and interacts with the audience. Example: Stand Up Comedy, asides.

REPRESENTATIONAL

When the reality of the audience is different than character or performer. The performer does not acknowledge or interact with the audience.

CHARACTERIZATION

The process of creating a character whose words and actions are determined by the elements of the play.

AD-LIB

Speech or action that is done by the actor within the context of the scene that has not been specifically written or rehearsed.

IMPROVISATION

Actor creates the scene in its entirety. Creation of who, what, when and where.

SUBTEXT

The underlying meaning to the scene not always apparent in the dialogue.

MOTIVATION

The character's reason for doing what he/she does within a moment, scene, act, or entire play.

INTNENTION

What the character wants from the other character(s) in a scene

PICKING UP CUES

When an actor is asked to shorten the time between when a cue is given and his/her response.

PRIMARY CHARACTER

The character that the story is about. "Macbeth" in the play Macbeth

SECONDARY CHARACTER

The Character that serves the story line. Provides information and action. For example, a messenger, butler, or confidant.

MONOLOGUE

One character speaking his/her lines either to themselves, another character, or the audience.

SOLILOQUY

A monologue that represents the inner workings of a character's mind. They speak out loud to themselves.

BEAT

A pause of varying length during a scene that is being played out. This beat is usually taken to emphasize emotion or thought or action.

If you are in an on camera acting class? These kinds of acting classes are very helpful if you want to get an idea of how you look on camera and how you are perceived by others. I do caution however, that the production elements of on camera classes are often deficient with poor lighting and sound. When you see your playback, you may have a skewed vision of yourself. Often students complain about the sound of their voices. But remember, poor sound makes your voice sound a lot worse than it is. On camera classes are a great way to see your physicality including the way you stand, gestures or mannerisms you may have that you were not aware existed. One common mannerism is leg slapping. Students will get up say a phrase, and then slap their sides of their legs as a form of dissipation of their nervousness. Another popular idiosyncrasy is the use of the word "um" in the middle of phrases. Something like this: "Hi, my name is Cyndi… um Smith… and I um want to take… um this class… um to learn um how to um act." Okay, I've overdone it a bit, but most people don't even know they do it. An on-camera class, then may be something to consider if it is available in your community. I am not expecting you to know all of these by memory, but some or all of them may be used in an on-camera class.

Basic Terminology for On Camera Acting

Who's Who on the Set

DIRECTOR

The person, who provides the point of view for the presentation of the play and directs the action.

AD or Assistant Director or First Assistant Director

Usually in charge of the crew – runs the set. Keeps order on the set and makes sure that production keeps moving.

Director: Second Assistant Director

Handle many details of production including calling actors, setting up actors and keeping the production on schedule.

Script Supervisor

Crew member who reads and times script as it is shot. This person also functions as a continuity person making sure the dialogue of the script is followed accurately by the actors.

SCREEN WRITER

A person who writes (DESCRIPTION, ACTION, DIALOGUE) in the form of a screenplay to be filmed.

DESIGNERS

People who create the "universe" of the film or television production - sound, lighting, costume, setting, props, special effects.

Production information - Words to know on the set

Action

Director's command to start.

Blocking the Shot

Usually done by the director. Carefully working out the movement and actions of actors and mobile television equipment.

Boom

The microphone is usually attached to the end of a long arm on a moveable platform.

Booth

Enclosed sound-proof area, separated from crew, with one or more microphones where actors can record the script (copy).

Camera Rehearsal

Full rehearsal with cameras and other pieces of production equipment in place to see how it all fits together.

Cheating

When an actor or object "angles" or faces toward a camera. Should be done so that it is not picked up by the audience.

Cue Card

Card with a portion of the script written on it in large letters. It is usually placed near the camera lens so that actors may read their lines. This is a common practice in soaps – with long sections of dialogue.

Cue

Signal in a script to start or stop any type of production activity or action.

Props – Personal (character)

Objects used by individual actors or characters in a film.

Props - Set

Furniture or other objects used for set decoration.

Props – Costume

Prop that usually belongs to a specific costume – scuba gear, or fox hunting outfit.

Script Supervisor

Crewmember who reads and times script as it is shot. This person also functions as a continuity person making sure the actors follow the dialogue of the script accurately.

Shot: Master Shot

A wide shot that shows the scene in its entirety.

Shot: Bust Shot

Shot of a single actor framed at bust.

Shot: Over the Shoulder

A shot in which we look across the back of one actor to the face of the other. Usually done in pairs so that the camera looks at both backs and both actors from similar but opposite points of view.

Shot: Matching

Usually, a master shot is done first. The actor must take special care to repeat almost exactly in the over the shoulder shots, close ups, and other coverage.

Shot: Waist Shot

Shot framed at the waist.

Shot: Dissolve

Shot double exposure between two scenes. Usually, the first scene is slowly replaced by the second one.

Shot: Full Shot

A full shot is framed at the feet or beyond.

Shot: Two Shot

Framing of two people.

Shot: Close-up (CU)

A shot of the actor's face, object or product taken at close range by the camera.

Slate

To identify verbally and visually before each take. A little black board (or white board) upon which essential production information is written (such as title, scene, date and take number.

Speed

Camera is running properly.

Take

Each time you shoot a scene is called a "take."

Teleprompter

Electrical device that displays the script in large letters that roll by in front of the camera lens at the speed of the actor's delivery.

Cut

Director's signal to stop the action.

Green Room

Waiting area for actors (historically painted green).

Hitting the Mark

Marks generally put on the floor to indicate the position of the actor's feet at the end of each move. Actors are expected to move to these marks without looking down at them.

It's a wrap

The end of production or shooting.

Pick up

When a director wants to re shoot a small portion of a scene

Playback

To replay (on a monitor) scenes or takes recorded in the studio.

Post-Production

Some on camera classes include some elements of what is called Post-Production.

Post-Production is the stage after **production** when the filming is completed and the editing and putting together of the visual and audio materials begins. From an acting standpoint that can include voice over narration, dubbing, and foley sound effects. The voice over and dubbing aspects of post-production are often covered in on-camera classes. As a beginning actor, it is a great way to explore your vocal placement and patterns of speech.

Post Production – Voice Over or ADR Script Directions

Dubbing

Replacing one voice or dialogue with another. (See also ADR)

ADRAutomatic Dialogue Replacement

When a voice actor replaces the voice of another actor or adds voices to a scene after it is shot.

Flap (Mouth Flap)

In animation or dubbing the movement of the mouth. If the talking stops and the character's mouth keeps moving. These are the movements of the character's mouth that must be filled by the actor's dialogue.

Lip Sync

Synchronization of sound and lip movement. (See also ADR and Dubbing)

Looping

Providing additional dialogue or sweetening for a scene (See also ADR)

MNS

Mouth not seen – direction often used in dubbing or voice over where the subject's mouth is not scene in frame.

MOS

A take without sound. Derived from early German Director's "mitout sound."

REAX

Reactions – direction often used in dubbing or voice over.

Sweeten

To enrich the background often with music, dialogue, or sound effects. (See also Looping, ADR and M/E)

Sync Sound

Synchronizing sound with picture.

“

Words mean more than what is set down on paper. It takes the human voice to infuse them with deeper meaning

Maya Angelo

CHAPTER 7
What Happens in an Acting Class?

Okay, you are now part of a Beginning acting class, what can you expect to do there? After your initial break the ice discussion (depending upon the type of class you are enrolled in) you might participate in several types of activities.

Improvisation:

Acting teachers like to start acting classes with improvisation because it is a great way to get beginning students to participate in acting exercises. There are no lines to memorize. Instead, you can be given some detail such as a character, situation, a word or a physical gesture and then asked to create a reality around it. Your teacher may ask you to participate in a two person or larger group scenario and perform an improvisation or exercise to help you get more comfortable performing. Don't fall into the trap of trying to think of something funny to say. By the time you think of it, the scene and physicality will have changed. Just play this moment to moment. Here are a few examples from many different sources including Viola Spolin's book *Improvisation for the Theatre – New Albany Press (2013).*

Tag Scene:

Done with the entire class in a circle. Two performers in the center are given circumstances to begin. The suggestion could be as simple as a person checking out at the grocery store. As the improvised scene begins, the other class members watch, and soon as the characters are established, someone from the class member yells "freeze!" The actors in the center freeze in whatever position they were in, and the actor who called freeze runs into the center of the circle, tags (or taps) one of the actors out and assumes their exact physical position. Then, starts an entirely new scene by saying a new first line with new characters and situation. Sometimes, I do this scene with students being assigned a specific first line. This forces them out of the habit of not participating because they can't come up with something funny. Tag scenes can go on continuously with different people tagging in and out of scenes.

First Line:

Two actors are given a random first line and begin an improvised scene. One participant begins the scene with the line and then the two together slowly build a who, what, when and where for the scene. Once it is established, the teacher usually stops at the scene. Don't fall into the trap of being literal. If you get a line that's absurd, something like, "That's my banana." You don't have to make the banana a banana. It can be anything, a pet, a car, a painting… be creative.

First Line Last Line (Concentration)

This is the same as the first line scene, usually with two actors. The only difference is that you will start the scene with a specific first line and then establish the who, what, when and where and then create a believable ending for the scene using the specific last line.

Yes but… (agree/disagree)

This exercise focuses on listening to one another and setting objectives. As the scene begins, one actor will enter with a certain physicality and objective. The other actor will agree to a certain aspect but then disagree with another. An example would be two characters sitting at a bus stop and one establishes that it is hot while the other takes the opposite stance and says it cold. As I write this, I am thinking of the famous Monty Python skit called "The Argument

https://www.youtube.com/watch?v=ohDB5gbtaEQ

Stand Sit and Lay (concentration)

This is an exercise in concentration. The setup for this improvisation is with three performers who may be given a line or a situation to play. During the scene each performer must be sitting, standing, or lying down. Each time a performer changes their physical state, the other two must change theirs. For example, if one character is standing while talking then sits down. The character that is sitting must either stand or lay down. This three-way evolution of the scene continues until the situation is resolved or the teacher ends it.

Motivation

This is an excellent improvisation which trains you to focus on getting something that you want. It could be getting a job, selling something, trying to leave a situation, asking for something, or making a request. It is usually set up with two performers, with one having the motivation of wanting something and the other a blank page as far as accepting or rejecting the request. This exercise enables the performer to work on all three aspects of performance including physicality, emotion, and intellect during their presentation. The interesting part one can experience during this exercise is the disconnect between the three basic elements of communication. Let's say the scene is a job interview and the person being interviewed says all the right things (intellectual) and has a confident demeanor (emotion) but has arms folded and is hunched over (physicality). In this example, the physicality is not in sync with the other two elements. The goal is to get all three working together and this is an excellent exercise in learning how to do this in the real world.

Subtext (What is really going on?)

This is a valuable exercise for you to learn. Often what people say and physically do is the opposite of what really is happening. We see this accentuated when politicians make speeches, but on an interpersonal level, this might be harder to interpret. An example might be if there are two characters speaking and Character #2 sits with arms folded with a sour angry expression.

CHARACTER #1

Are you mad at me?

CHARACTER #2

I'm fine.

CHARACTER #1

It just seems like you are angry.

CHARACTER #1

I said, I'm fine.

In this simple example, the lines or words say one thing and the emotion and physicality say another. How many times have you done this when you are upset about something in life? The subtext of this scene is that one character is angry at another for some reason, but the dialog says the opposite. This is what subtext is concerned with, and in your dealings with other people in your life you must be sensitive to what the subtext or what is really going on in your situation.

Be an Animal (physicality)

This is not one of my favorite exercises because students tend to create a physical caricature of the animal they are trying to assume. They often create an exaggerated version of the animal they assume. The exercise is not asking you to be the animal, but rather asking you to assume some of the physical characteristics of an animal and embody those characteristics with a human character. Let's take the example of a monkey. You might, as a human character take on some of the erratic physical traits of a monkey.

But it is not a valuable exercise if you swing from the chandelier screaming with a banana in your hand. There is a difference. If you were to create a human character around an animal, then, you might take some of the physical characteristics of that animal and apply them with the human character's physicality. Think of your family members or people you might know at work and picture one of them in your mind. What kind of animal do they most emulate? I have one colleague that reminds me of a velociraptor dinosaur when I see him walking down the hallway. He's hunched over and grimaces so you can see his teeth and looks like he's hunting for prey. This exercise can be a great way to get people to loosen up if they are nervous about getting up and performing. Playing an animal allows them to hide themselves behind the vocal and physical gestures of the animal they are playing. But aside from that fact, this kind of exercise usually becomes a series of exaggerated and comic gestures and won't connect you to any specific reality. I don't want you to go to an audition, your workplace or home making gestures like an animal.

Mirror or Opposite (physicality)

This is a valuable exercise, especially for people in sales. Mirroring **in sales** is the practice where the salesperson mirrors or imitates the verbal or nonverbal behaviors of the person they are trying to get to do something. It could be anything from selling a product or service. The idea is that you want the other person or prospect to feel comfortable, so you you become them. The opposite physicality is something you should be more aware of when trying to communicate. If you are requesting a day off or a raise and your boss has legs crossed and arms folded, this is a physical signal that they don't want to give you what you want. In an acting class, you could be given a scenario (situation) and asked to mirror them or do the opposite. Remember, it's not exactly science. If they fold their arms and you are asked to mirror them, don't immediately fold your arms. Instead, communicate an idea and then slowly get to the physicality and behavior that mirrors their position. If you are tasked with the opposite, work slowly to get them to mirror you. If someone doesn't want to give you what you want, stay with them, wear them down until they give in just like a good salesperson would do. As a beginning actor mirroring is a great way to establish your character in relationship with other characters in a scene. This was done in the motion picture Mean Girls, where the plastics and nerds all looked and acted alike.

One Word at a Time (physicality and concentration)

This is a great exercise to work on concentration. It essentially is asking you to communicate in each set of circumstances using only one word at a time. This would mean that if it were a two-person improvisation, you could only communicate to the other character using one word at a time. The challenge here is to use physicality to communicate what you normally just say verbally. Using one word at a time also sharpens your concentration skills. Remember, you would have the challenge of moving the scene forward toward completion one word at a time.

Questions Only (physicality and concentration)

In this exercise you may only ask questions. This is a similar challenge to moving the scene forward, but only by asking questions. This a great way to learn concentration and how to move a particular situation forward by combining physicality to verbal communication. Think about the times you have walked into a sales situation while looking at a car, and you are immediately faced with a series of questions.

SALESPERSON

Can I help you?

YOU

Is browsing, okay?

SALESPERSON

Yes, what are you looking for?

YOU

Not sure, what do you think about a convertible?

SALESPERSON

Great! Are you ready to make a purchase today?

YOU

What colors do you have?

SALESPERSON

If I give you a good price, will you buy today?

YOU

Maybe, what can you tell me about that red convertible?

Physical Action into a Scene:

You might be asked to start a scene with a specific physical action instead of a word. The action could be something literal like sawing a log, or something abstract like moving your right arm up and down. The most important thing with this physical action is that it must be repeated

You cannot start the scene by just doing a group of unrelated and unrepeated actions. The improvisation then begins out of that repeated physical action, which can evolve into a single word, a sentence, or an alternate physical action. Once the process has started, the scene is created slowly until the characters and situation are developed.

I could go on here for an extreme length listing all the variations of different types of improvisations that you might encounter when you begin an acting class. The important thing about improvisation within an acting class is that it's an opportunity for you to get on a stage or in front of a camera or in a group and perform a character, a situation or presentation. My only caution is, don't be pulled into the trap of trying to be funny. What normally happens is there is a series of what I will call ONE-UPS where people will try to be funnier than the previous person or group that went before. It's an escalation that really goes nowhere and really forces students not to participate because they are always trying to think of what to do or say to top off the last funny moment. Also, there's always going to be one or two people in your class, whether it's live, face to face or online, that are going to be naturally funny. And what will happen is they will dominate the exercises which prevents other students from participating because they will feel intimidated by their sense of comedy. Incidentally, this can happen in a work environment as well; you could have one person that dominates all the activities, and the way work is conducted at your job. And I don't mean your boss, I mean someone that's a coworker who will draw all the attention to them on almost every issue. This makes it very difficult for you to be noticed or participate in what's going on in your work environment. Think of improvisation as a give and take process. The best way to learn improvisation is to go moment to moment and truly improvise and create on the spot characters, physicality and situations.

Monologues - What is a monologue?

The American Heritage Dictionary defines a monologue as a long speech made by one person, often monopolizing a conversation. You may be thinking, I already know that I have relatives that do that all the time. Tell me something I don't know and why I would need to know monologue? Okay, a monologue when spoken can reveal a small part of a character's soul. Think of those thoughts in which you have spoken aloud to someone or yourself. The words you speak come from within you and have special meaning. Unless, you count as monologues leaving phone messages, placing your order at the automated machine at Jack in the Box or trying to talk on the phone to customer service at your bank. It is true that a monologue is a speech made by one person, but really it is a lot more than just that. What the person says in his/her speech should be worthy of speech itself to be considered a monologue. A monologue should be a speech connected in some core way to your character's intellectual, emotional, spiritual, and physical state. If it is not that, then it is not a monologue. It is whatever it is: leaving a phone message, ordering a cheeseburger, or trying to find out why your check has bounced.

Within the framework of an acting class or performing arts presentation, a monologue is one person speaking for an extended period alone, with other characters upon the stage or to an audience on a stage or within a camera shot. The speech can be the character's thoughts spoken aloud to himself or herself, to another character, to the audience, or to an object. How a monologue is presented has a lot to do with the reality of the universe the character lives in and to a greater extent the point of view or creative framework of the presentation. I am defining a point of view as ***how*** a creative work is presented to its audience. Several years ago, I attended a production of William Shakespeare's Hamlet at a small theatre in Los Angeles. I sat in the first row about three feet from the actor who played Hamlet as he uttered those famous lines ***"To be or not to be..."*** I had experienced this soliloquy dozens of times before within a representational framework where the Hamlet character reveals his inner thoughts by speaking to himself out loud. In this production, the actor who played Hamlet looked directly at me and asked the famous question, "To ***be or not to be?"*** At first, I wanted to blurt out, like Robert Di Niro in ***Taxi Driver, "Are you talking to me?"*** But, somehow thought it might not be appropriate. I said nothing. But I did give him a look of acknowledgment. As if to say, "I ***heard that... and that is definitely a question to consider."*** For the rest of the show, the audience kept looking at me as if they wanted me to do or say something. I never did. I am not saying that it was wrong to present Hamlet's soliloquy in this manner. The creative framework of that production of Hamlet was *"presentational,"* meaning it had the characters (including Hamlet) acknowledging the presence of the audience. At that performance I unwittingly assumed that role. I could have chosen to respond verbally to Hamlet, but I chose just to acknowledge his look.

However, we can say that Hamlet acknowledging the audience in the middle of his soliloquy was done on purpose and was part of the creative framework of the presentation. The creative framework, which defines a presentation of a play or film to an audience, usually falls within the point of view of the Director.

The director of a play or film sets the framework and tone of how the material will be presented. When you choose to perform a particular monologue, just like a director, you must choose ***how*** you will convey the reality of your character and situation to an audience. You must ask yourself, what do I want to achieve within my creative framework and what is the desired outcome? I am not suggesting that you perform your acting class monologue directly to your teacher or classmates. I think it is best to create a framework that keeps them separate from the reality of your character. This allows the teacher to make notes on your performance, sit back, and see what you can do, and it enables your classmates to observe you without being part of the presentation. You don't want them; feeling forced to react to your gaze or directed line toward them. It will make them uncomfortable and lessen your chance to showcase what you can do. Your creative framework in presenting your monologue should be focused on how to best present the reality of the character you have created within a given universe and to connect that character to your individual talents. The purpose of an acting class monologue is not to solely show your acting ability; it should also illustrate how you create a character, interpret lines, and present them to an audience.

Now that we have discussed what a monologue is and how it should be presented, let's get back to our original question. Why do we have to do monologues in an acting class anyway?

For the purposes of an acting class, many acting teachers assign monologues to their incoming students to get an idea of their skill level. Also, some teachers like to assign monologues right up front in the first or second meeting to get an idea of the level of skills a new student possesses and as a method to weed any new students that don't want to fully participate in the class. Remember a monologue is something that must be memorized, and if a student is not serious about learning how to do that or afraid of that requirement, they often drop the class. But why would you need to look to take a monologue class? Like a commercial, which is a thirty-second presentation, a monologue is about getting an idea to an audience. Monologues should be about a minute to a minute and a half presenting a character or situation and providing the audience with an opportunity to understand. This is an important skill for you to learn. How to make a presentation or communicate an idea to a coworker or supervisor. I'm not saying that you need to perform before your coworkers or supervisors, but it's a way for you to clarify what you're trying to accomplish and want at your workplace. For these reasons, performing a monologue is a valuable skill to learn. If you are assigned a monologue in your acting class, don't be afraid of memorizing the lines. Select a monologue that is no longer than one minute. There will be several monologues attached to this book so that you will have them available to you should you need it.

Cold Reading or Scene Classes

There are two other types of classes and I'm, lumping them together here, but I'm going to define them separately, so you know the difference between the two.

Cold Reading Classes

A cold reading class could also be called an audition class and its real focus is to prepare the actor for reading and performing a script for a possible audition. It's called cold reading, but, there's very little cold about cold readings. A cold reading is essentially a monologue or a scene which is used for an audition. When I say it is for an audition, I also want you to know that the pages that are read are usually from a specific film, television show or play that is being cast. It is not a separate script, but rather selects pages from the project that is being created. The cold reading pages are called "sides" and they refer to selections of the script being produced. They are almost always selected by character. Sides often contain specific pages or segments of a script where one character is speaking with another, and you would then prepare that character. Usually, the character's name is written at the top of the side pages. But with modern technology, cold readings have not been cold for many years. Before the internet, actors would go to a casting office and at that location receive a hard copy of several pages from a script. They would have a brief period in the casting office for a quick look at it and then go in and perform those side pages for a casting director, director, or producer. That is why the reading was called cold, because there was very little time for the actor to prepare or memorize the script. Fast forward to modern technology and all script material for auditions is made available online to actors before the audition and often provided by an agent days before the actor goes in for what they call a reading. They still call it cold reading, but it really isn't because the actor now can familiarize themselves with the script memorize it and then perform it in front of a casting director. Actors still hold the pages in their hands most of the time when they go in. but they know the script by heart and use a elements of eye contact and physicality which they wouldn't be able to do as well if they didn't know the script. Having the sides beforehand allows actors the opportunity to make specific choices based on their talent and what they believe the casting directors or producers want for that character. It is essentially a scene class, and you would go in and sometimes more than often perform in front of a camera and you'd get an opportunity to see yourself. Also, a cold reading class would provide a series of short scenes which you may get right on the spot in your class and then perform them either face to face or online. This is a great way to learn how to present material with little or no preparation, so this could be a good thing for you. Cold reading classes are often short in duration and many of them are offered with only one meeting over an afternoon, or some of them meet two or three times and they may do dramatic, comedy or commercial presentations. Performing commercial copy on the spot will help you focus and prepare you to present a concept in under 30 seconds. A cold reading class would be a valuable class for you to learn how to conceptualize material for a presentation before a live or recorded audience period

Scene Study

Some acting classes focus on the presentation of scenes from plays, movies, or television shows. Most of the time these scenes have two characters in them and run from as little as one or two minutes to 10 minutes. The purpose of a scene presentation in a class is to present a character in a particular situation and your ability to work with another person in a performance.

What is a scene?

I think it's important to understand exactly what you are presenting when you select material to perform. The minimal answer is that a scene is a set number of pages from a play or film script that contain ACTION, DESCRIPTION and DIALOGUE. Also, that within those set number of pages, actors must establish a WHO, WHAT, WHERE, WHEN and WHY reality for the characters and actions contained in them. Students often bring scenes into my classes that fail to establish even a few of the criteria that we have established above. They often have the characters down and the characters speak, but there is no reason for them to speak or do anything for that matter. So, they become talking heads struggling in a vacuum because they have nothing to act. When I ask them why their character did what he/she did? They reply, "***Because that's the way it was in the movie.***" They operate at a disadvantage if that is the criteria they have chosen. Whatever they have seen from a movie has been edited with music and effects added and are quite a different performance dynamic that presenting in an audition or class. When they use a movie, or something clip from YouTube as a reference that does not take into consideration that one scene which appears in a movie may be a small fragment of a larger scene. The students present the fragment as a stand-alone in class and it may only run forty-five seconds, and nothing happens. Why? It is incomplete. If you do a fragment of a scene as part of an audition, these pages have been selected by the casting director for specific reasons. sides in a cold reading, the casting director has selected the material for very specific reasons, which may not require a whole interpretation. However, as an actor, you should have an idea of how the part you are performing relates to the whole. It might mean reading the entire script to give meaning to the two-minute scene you are performing. A producer once asked me if I ever dipped a piece of bread in a cooking pot of tomato sauce. I wasn't sure if I did or not, but I told him I did. Then he smiled and said, if you stir the pot, and take a small taste, shouldn't it be representative of the whole pot? I'm getting hungry writing this, but you get my message. The scene, even though a small taste, must be representative of the entire work. Let's look at what a scene can be so that you can know what to act on and how to put it together for an audition or an acting class. The American Heritage Dictionary definition states:

A scene is something seen by a viewer or prospect:

This is often forgotten when a scene is presented. Actors have the tendency to focus inwardly on their character and forget that they are presenting material for an audience. Always ask yourself, where is the audience and how can I frame the situation and action so that they can be involved in it intellectually and emotionally?

A scene is the place where an action or event occurs:

When creating the reality of the moment in your scene, don't forget to also establish the universe that your character is living within. Your character will have to react to that universe, and it influences the "how" and "why" they do what they do within the scene.

A scene is the place in which the action of a play, movie or other narrative occurs:

This is the literal location. The house, the living room, the study etc.... but it is so much more. It's not just about the literal location or setting of the action. What is specific about the space? What is its ownership? If you were to set a scene in the middle of the night at a graveyard – that would be one location. But what if you were to set a scene in the middle of the night at a graveyard, standing over a grave with your character's name on it. Is the grave empty or does it have someone in it? If so, who? This location would change the emotional center of a character within a scene. The place can also be somewhere other than the literal location of the character within a scene. In Anton Chekov's play, THREE SISTERS, Irina, the youngest of the three, longs to go to Moscow. Although the actual location of the play is not in Moscow, Irina's hopes, and dreams all live there. This is where she emanates from. So, a place within a scene can be many things.

A scene is a subdivision of an act in a dramatic presentation in which the setting is fixed and the time continuous:

A scene, if it is part of a play, is like one tile in a mosaic. It has its own beginning, middle, and end, which is connected to a larger narrative.

When you perform your scene, even if it is a stand-alone, you must incorporate the reality of the larger narrative. It doesn't mean you have to perform the entire play, but you must consider where your scene falls within the larger context. Ask yourself, as your scene begins, what moment or event has triggered the initial moment you are playing at the start of your action.

A scene is a shot or series of shots in a movie making up a unit of continuous related action:

In film, the location can change so the setting is not fixed. Also, film is usually shot out of order, so while the same theory applies pertaining to a linear narrative, film is more visual and moves back and forth within time frames and action. You still must play the larger narrative; however, you need to be aware of how and in what order that narrative is written in the body of the screenplay. Performing a scene is a lot more than just two characters facing each other and talking. It is also, a bit more than simply playing who, what, when, where and why? You really must look at the whole piece that the scene emanates from to truly understand then convey the "why." Now, let's think about how a scene study class is going to meet your needs as a beginning actor.

Now that I have described what a scene is, doesn't this remind you of situations that may arise out of your personal experience at home or workplace? Think of the last time you asked for something at your workplace that occurred between you and another person. How would you describe your character? Were you strong and clear in describing what you needed or were you weak and vague because you did not want the person you were asking to be angry at you? A scene study class is an excellent way for you to hone your skills in communicating in relationships with people. Also, a great way to get an understanding of the character that you may play in the universe you are operating in. Remember, you are a beginning actor using what you have learned in class to create a character with clear cut motivation so they can achieve what they want.

Motivation:

Your character's motivation is ***what drives them or what they would like to achieve****. For example, a character may behave in a childish or argumentative way, but their overall motivation is to be noticed and get attention.*

https://lisbdnet.com/what-does-character-motivation-mean/

Characters do what they do in each play or movie because they are motivated to do so. A simple example might be a police detective trying to track down and catch a murderer. Everything that character does within that universe is focused on that one thing, and we watch it when we watch a movie or a television show. The final scene usually shows the murderer being brought to justice and making it all right. Use these same techniques when you perform, at home and in your workplace. You may not reach your goal right away, but the important thing is to keep improving and trying.

“

Don’t take yourself too seriously. Know when to laugh at yourself, and find a way to laugh at obstacles that inevitably present themselves.

”

Halle Berry

CHAPTER 8

Who are You?

When you look at yourself in the mirror, you know who you are. But the way you define yourself is disconnected from how you are perceived by others. You must have a clear idea of who you are and how you are perceived by others within a particular universe. As an actor, who you are, your experiences, beliefs and physicality are your palette that you will draw upon when creating a character. You bring all of this with you when you perform on stage or in front of a camera. Your life experience is your own play or movie. Stop here

Each universe you enter into in your own life is like a play or a film and you are a character in it. From that perspective it's more about how you are perceived within that universe or work environment that you want to try to understand. Also, one of the key areas of interrelating with other people in a specific environment is whether you understand how you are perceived. Often many times I have students in my classes that have a disconnect between how they are perceived by others and how they perceive themselves. It's important to have these two perceptions in total synchronization. Also, if you don't like how, you are perceived by others, you can always change. It takes time to achieve this, but it can be accomplished. Our goal at this moment is to look at you in a particular universe or work environment and try to define who you are and more specifically, how others define you. Let’s divide your universe into several parts. Choose the ones that apply to you.

With family

With friends

At work/office

Meeting new people

Alone

Then break each part down into four integral character attribute components

Intellectual

Emotional

Physical

Spiritual

Select each universe and define each component within it as if you were a character in a play or movie. This would be the same process by which you would define a character you would play in a film or theater production if you were acting in it. Let's define these four-character attributes components which are part of an acting class and then apply them to your specific universes.

Intellectual:

This is what your character intellectually believes to be so within his/her universe. It goes to the core of their beliefs and the things they do. It could be as simple as Democrat or Republican, but it can go deeper about their understanding of the universe, they live in. Characters are often thrust into situations that force them to make decisions based upon logic rather than emotion. This is often the case in business decisions where statistics or numbers are involved. However, an intellectual choice can also be based upon a belief system within the character. Some factor causes your character to calculate and then act upon a decision centered around facts and data rather than feelings. In a work environment, it would detail how much or how little you would know about your specific job and your work universe in general. As a family, it might be how you budget your expenses.

Emotional:

In a play or movie, this is what your character feels about themselves and the other characters they relate to in their universe. What emotion dominates their existence and how does it affect what they do and what happens to them. Certain situations demand an emotional response. What you feel becomes more important than what your character thinks or intellectually rationalizes in each situation. In 1916, there was a shark attack on a little boy in an inland Florida lagoon. It was unbelievable to think that a shark could swim that far inland from the ocean. But it happened. As the shark attacked the seven-year-old, an adult man jumped into the water and tried to pull him to safety. The shark killed them both, but there is more to it than that. The underlying motivation for the rescuer was to save the boy despite the danger of being torn apart himself. It was fear itself that drew the man into the water. This was the incident that inspired the JAWS movie and was based upon an emotional response.

In your work/office universe definition, emotion is more about showing than it is telling. You wouldn't say using the same example, "Hello my name is Fred and I'm a very happy person working in accounting." Emotion can essentially be your state of mind and body now as you meet a new person within that universe. The "go to" emotional choice within a work/office universe is usually happy, enthusiastic, eager, or caring. It can also be critical, negative, annoyed, or angry. When you meet a new person, be warm and friendly and listen to what they say about themselves and their own point of view and their position. As an actor, find points to make positive connections to all other people in your universe.

Physicality

In a play or movie, how does your character physically interact with the universe they live in? How do they move? How do they interact physically with other characters? Are they open, relaxed and strong or hunched, arms tightly folded and closed? Our physical response to the world is filtered through our culture and the times we live in. It says many things about who we are. You could be in a subway car in New York City, just inches away from another individual. So close to them that you could smell what they ate for breakfast but not think anything of it because of the close physicality of that space. You could take the same physical situation as waiting in a line at the supermarket in Los Angeles and you would sense anyone that close to you as invading your space. A character's physical interaction with the universe that surrounds them can also be influenced by culture or period. What is acceptable in one culture or period may not be acceptable in another.

In your family universe, you are physically relaxed as you operate the different parts you play as mother, father, daughter, son, or sibling. In your work world, physicality like emotion, is something that you're going to show rather than tell. You will hear that very same message spoken by your acting teachers that you should "show" instead of "tell." Certain circumstances, events or universe spaces require certain physicality. In your professional universe, you should physically interact with people differently than you would in your home universe. Auditions, business meetings, are different than meeting friends for a coffee. Your physicality must be in sync with your emotional state. If you are warm and friendly, then your physical appearance and physical state should be the same. What does this mean? Your physicality says a lot about who you are and that is why we discuss it in this chapter. I want you to focus on being present in the space but not being overbearing. What defines overbearing? Overbearing would be talking too loud or too close, invading their personal space or touching a person. You don't have to be the dominant person in every new conversation. Instead, be a friendly person who is approachable so that people will want to know more about you. How is this achieved? If you are warm and friendly you will keep a normal distance, and you will not exert any physical pressure by touching people you have just met. Be firmly in control of your immediate surroundings and make sure that you're not withdrawn or with arms folded or by gazing at areas such as the ceiling or the floor. Physicality is important because it reveals more about a person than what they say. If I see someone in a space being loud or too physical, it tells me that there's a certain level of insecurity surrounding that individual. When you meet a person for the first-time being loud and overbearing is not the kind of image you want to portray if you want to show strength. Instead, be open, physically, listen and learn about the person you are meeting for the first time and give them time so that they might learn something about you. An acting class can strengthen your ability to control your physicality and learn how to maneuver in real-life environments. What about spirituality?

Spiritual:

In an acting class, what are your characters' values which go beyond religious conviction to the core of their belief system? Your character's moral core and how they perceive what is just and unjust within their universe. Certain characters find themselves on a voyage of discovery and their motivation is centered on that journey. Certainly, Don Quixote's quest in Man of La Mancha would be an example. But your character doesn't have to be on a life-long quest to find the meaning of life to have a spiritual motivation. Spirituality can simply be an exploration of an aspect of your character's inner being.

Certainly, try to allow whomever your character is speaking to react to what is being conveyed just as you would in a two-person scene. Your character speaks the lines in the monologue and then allows the other character or the audience to respond. Even if they are not making a sound, you need to give them time to react. If you do this, your presentation will be more than a mere recitation of the words of the script in which you race through the lines before you forget them. Allow whomever you are speaking to, to absorb what you are saying and doing. Also, don't forget to create them in the space. Look at them, react to them, and allow them to react to what your character is doing within the piece.

In your world, spirituality is something abstract in many ways and not as literal as intellectual, emotional, or physical attributes. Your spirituality really reflects the kind of person you are, how you view your universe and what is important to you. When I think of qualities of spirituality, I think of honesty, peace responsibility, and trustworthiness. These are all attributes that you want to reflect as your own when you meet new people. How do you accomplish this has to be something that you really feel or believe about the universe? It is not a religious statement. Spirituality reflects your values, how you see the world and how you treat the people that you interact with in your universe. That would be a spirituality that is positive, one that people would want to be around. Individuals with a high spirituality are also people that others trust and that is something that you want to be able to project. This means that you take on responsibilities and if you make mistakes, you admit them and learn from them and always have a positive objective in mind. You can project a solid spirituality onto any new person that you meet and validate relationships with individuals you already know.

Meeting someone for the first time in your acting class

So now that you have defined yourself, how do you describe yourself to other members of your acting class? I want you to think about when you meet a person one-on one for the first time you say your name and follow how you are connected to the acting class. How do you interact and describe yourself to someone who doesn't know you? I want you to think of three different terms **professional, personal and private**. If you were in an acting class and had to perform a cold reading, you would not have the benefit of the entire script to define your character. Remember, a cold reading will be performed in an abbreviated format with only a few pages available to make specific choices for your performance. A brief introduction at an event, is a similar type of configuration. You meet someone for the first time and only for a few moments. How do you introduce yourself using the three "p's" professional, personal, and private? Let's define these as the three "p's."

Professional:

What you do to earn a living. In an acting class, you can establish that you are a working actor. However, as a beginning actor it is more likely what you do to earn money outside acting. If you are a student, it would be your major. Are you an insurance salesperson, homemaker, or schoolteacher? If you put an adjective in front of any of those professional choices, it changes everything. It could be you stating your name and what department or division you work in at a large company. If your name is John and you work in the accounting department, you might change your introduction to be more specific by stating your name and then a particular function you do within that department. "Hello, my name is John and I work on the distribution and finance agreements for all motion pictures at this studio." You are describing your position with more focus for someone who is trying to figure out what you do. People you meet for the first time also want to know what you do so they can assess whether you can support them in what they want to achieve. Now I'm going to pause for this definition just to say one thing. If you have a career goal and the job that you have is just a job to pay your bills until you get to your goal, you need to include your big picture goal as much as you can to provide a better idea of who you are. For example, "Hello my name is John I'm a graduate student in film and I'm working in the finance department for motion pictures and television." You do this because you want people to have a more accurate vision of who you really are. Providing a bit more detail, you will find points of connection between the person you are meeting for the first time and yourself. The more detail and definition you can provide in your introduction, the more the opportunity for you to connect with an individual on a different level than just saying hello how do you do I work in accounting, or I am a student. Stay away from politics or criticizing the people you work with or the company universe you work in. Don't say, "Hello my name is John and I'm only working a company x which is a rat hole until I'm out of graduate school in filmmaking and after that I'm gone." Your introduction should really be about connecting on a professional level with new people and secondly, trying to find similarities in those connections that you can build upon. After people meet you and they know what you do, what do they want to know next?

Personal:

In an acting class or cold reading when performing, you would want to reveal something personal about your character and how that connect drives the choices you create when portraying them. In cold reading, the personal state of the character drives everything they do within the play or movie. In life as a student in an acting class, personal is something about you and your connections to people outside the universe of the class. New people you meet, will want to know if you are married, divorced, single, available, or not available, and if you are related to someone within the universe of the acting class. You may not want to share your personal relationships with someone you don't know at a first-time meeting. That's fine, but there will always be a thought in their mind of what your personal relationships are both outside and within the universe of the class. How much or how little you share that is up to you. What about secrets about you to create a sense of mystery?

Private:

In cold reading for a live play or film, when a character breakdown is presented both for professional, personal, and private purposes, it is done to create a very interesting character. The private aspect of a character is known only by the character when they are alone. In an acting class environment as a beginning actor, you might want to create an air of mystery when meeting someone new. People always want to know more about what is unknown. This is not to say that you're going to act strangely, but that your private moments might be reflected in the way you talk about a particular topic or your physical demeanor. Most of the time when meeting a person for the first time it is best just to be warm and friendly and leave the private part for a later. But I did want to mention it because it is also part of what actors use in creating choices to present a character.

“

Our true character is that person we become when no one is watching.

”

Unknown

CHAPTER 9

Your First Acting Assignments
Monologues and Scenes

What's the best way to memorize my lines and create a physical life for my character?

I have heard many student actors complain: ***"I knew the lines outside in my car or in my house but now, on the stage, I just can't remember anything."*** When I hear this statement, I know what they have forgotten to do is create a physical life for their character. They fall into the trap of thinking about their scene as just a recitation of lines rather than a slice of a character's life. The moment that we experience your character speaking, it is part of a much larger mosaic. A play or film script contains three components which are available to an actor when performing a scene. They are DESCRIPTION, ACTION and DIALOGUE. What a lot of actors concentrate on is dialogue. They try to memorize lines as a speech and do nothing else. When they stand on stage or in front of a camera, they try to remember this isolated dialogue and suddenly everything goes blank. This is because they have forgotten to include description and action. To make matters worse, they learn dialogue within a physicality that has nothing to do with the reality of the scene they will perform. They work on lines while driving in their car (sometimes on the way to class), watching television or lying down on a couch. Then, when they get on their feet for the first time, their brain cannot connect to the new physicality.

When preparing to perform your first monologue or scene, don't forget the description of your character and the setting. Also pay attention to what is written about the physical life of the character. What I mean is the physical connection to where your character is and what they are doing as they speak. Creating a physical life will go a long way in helping you to memorize the lines. Your ability to memorize what your character is saying will be connected to a specific physical reality and idea. Your brain will connect what is spoken to a specific movement and place. However, you cannot move without purpose. What kind of universe does your character live in and how do they move within it? A character's universe has everything to do with the actual space from which they speak, the period they live in, and ***who*** they are speaking to. All this preparation should be done before you perform on a stage in front of an audience or in front of a camera. Try as best as you can to rehearse a monologue with someone watching or with your scene partner.

How to create an implementation strategy that works

Think of an implementation strategy as a plan to create a frame or foundation to build and present your monologue or scene. The implementation strategy becomes the concept for presentation. Whatever the purpose of your preparation for presentation should include an implementation strategy. You may think it is the director's job to create the framework for the character's physicality and emotion and that you should not have to concern yourself with the details of how it will be presented. The truth is that the ***who and the how*** are connected. It is like the chef who labors over the preparation and ingredients, making up a particular dish, forgetting presentation and just throwing their creation onto a paper plate. In that very act, the chef negates the creative process that has taken place before. An actor is no different; consideration of presentation is just as important as character preparation. While an actor cannot control all aspects of presentation, the development of an implementation strategy will create a foundation for the actor to rely upon.

Creating a performance dynamic - How to create a creative box to play in

The dynamic of any presentation considers all the physical characteristics of the performance space, the performer's relationship to that space, the distance of the intended audience to the performer, the composition of the intended audience, the surrounding reality of the performance and ultimately the purpose of the performance itself. The dynamics of any given performance can change as the physical characteristics of the space change. While it is virtually impossible for any performer to totally know the dynamic of every class performance in advance, it is possible to develop a strategy for presentation, based upon what elements are available.

For an acting class, you should be somewhat familiar with the dynamics of the studio space and the distance you will be from your audience. Also, find out where the light is within that space. Is it general lighting or like many acting studios do, several fixed spotlights light the space? Try to find the light and create your action within that space. Students have presented monologues or scenes for performing in my acting classes and set them at the darkest part of the stage. I often must reset the scene before they begin so that it takes place in the light and can be seen by the rest of the class. You have a general knowledge of the space, so use that information. That is not always the case in an audition.

For an audition, you can only assume the dynamics of the space and distance to the intended audience. You might have to present your monologue or scene in an office setting, a conference room, or an empty stage. The best strategy is to prepare a plan for all three. In an audition dynamic, the person you are auditioning for may be looking for a specific element and not your total performance. They also may be multi-tasking (making notations, conferring with an associate, or looking at your resume) while you are in the midst of your performance. Lastly, the reality you try to create might be interrupted by an outside source, such as a telephone, person entering the space or the casting person themselves.

The ***Presentation Dynamic*** is literally the creative box you get to play in. It is the creative framework, which is made up of your character's world, and the physical elements within your specific performance environment all rolled into one. It could be a stage space, an outdoor location, a camera angle, or a casting office that your character must evolve within. Caution, when presenting a scene for an acting class or an audition, try not to over-embellish the space to create a presentation dynamic. If your scene takes place in a restaurant, set up a table, chairs, utensils etc.... but you don't have to create the entire restaurant. Just focus on delineating the space so that it is clearly defined for an audience. Once you have established this creative framework, there is a multitude of possibilities that are present within that dynamic at that moment in time.

Using "What If?"

You have made the choices detailing **who, what, where and when**. Now, let your character ask him/herself the question: "***What If?"*** one of these choices weren't so? Example: You are Romeo quietly watching Juliet standing on her balcony.

Who: A Montague (who falls in and out of love) and enemy of the Capulets

What: Spying upon Juliet as she speaks her private thoughts

Where: Capulet's orchard, Verona - a place he should not be.

When: Nighttime after the Capulet feast.

Romeo sees the love of his life, but cannot muster the will to speak. As she speaks each line, he falls deeper and deeper into silence. He succumbs to his fear and gets up to run away when at the last possible moment, despite his fear, he hears Juliet say:

Romeo, doff thy name,

And for that name which is no part of thee

Take all myself!

When Romeo hears this, his fear vanishes in an instant, and he speaks! Why? He knows he can get it all.

I take thee at thy word:

Call me but love, and I'll be new baptized;

Henceforth I never will be Romeo

Using the "***What if?***' you are choosing to play the moment as if this time it will be different. You are playing this scene and speech as if he were going to walk away, and somehow this play, at this moment in time is different than any other that has happened before. The key to playing the "***what if?"*** is that your character must believe it, and more importantly, the audience must believe that the ***"what if?"*** is going to change the outcome. Fight the logical inclination to say to yourself, ***this is Shakespeare, or this is the text; it cannot be changed***. I am not suggesting a change in the text. Only a change in intention. We often play at the end of the scene because there is a preconceived notion by both performers and audiences as to how it all turns out. We need to recreate that notion in the form of "***what if?***" Let the audience sit on the edge of their seats and wonder if that maybe just this time, at this moment, Romeo just might walk away. What would happen then? Using this approach makes your work unpredictable and interesting.

How to play each moment as if it were a piece of a larger mosaic – and create the "MOMENT BEFORE"

Where have you come from and what has just happened the moment before?

Within the reality of your character, what moment has the character just left before they enter the moment your monologue or scene begins? What is significant about that moment and how will that moment influence the intellectual, emotional, physical, and spiritual state of your character? Within this creative framework, the actor then can convey the thoughts of the character, as they would appear in the full presentation of the work. Playing the moment before the lights go up or the camera rolls, then allows the audience to catch your character living their life in its entirety. The moment before propels your character into "NOW."

How to play each moment as if it were a piece of a larger mosaic - and create "NOW" using objectives and beats

What is your character's main objective?

By speaking the lines in a monologue or scene and living the moment, what does your character desire to have happen when the scene is over? Ask yourself, ***why*** is my character saying and doing this now? What is your character's desired outcome?

What are your character's sub-objectives? Mark them as individual beats.

Are there smaller objectives or beats your character must overcome to achieve their main objective? A beat could be a small section of the dialogue or movement within the scene. Create a series of beats within your scene to identify your sub-objectives. For example, what would Romeo's sub-objectives be?

Beat #1Romeo sees the love of his life on her balcony, but cannot muster the will to speak.

Beat #2 She says his name from her balcony. He succumbs to his fear and gets up to run away.

Beat #3At the last possible moment, despite his fear, he stops when he he hears Juliet say:

Romeo, doff thy name,

And for that name which is no part of thee

Take all myself!

Beat #5When Romeo hears this, his fear, vanishes in an instant.

Beat #6He speaks.

I take thee at thy word:

Call me but love, and I'll be new baptized;

Henceforth I never will be Romeo

What are the obstacles in the way of achieving your objectives?

In the course of events leading up to, during and after the completion of the monologue or scene, can you identify any obstacles, which are preventing your character from achieving his/her desired goals? Are these obstacles generated externally (literally physical elements) or internal (obstacles created from within your character) which prevent them from their objective? Identify these obstacles and create ways to acknowledge and overcome them.

What is going on NOW at this moment?

At the very moment the monologue or scene begins, what is happening? If you took a snapshot of this moment, what would be its title? If you enter your home holding a bouquet of flowers, kiss your wife and give them to her, and then after giving them to her, you tell her that you have lost your job, what is the title you would place under this moment? It can be called many things "***losing my job"*** or ***"loss"*** but it would not be called "***Giving her the bouquet"*** because that action is not what is really going on. It is just an action, which is part of the overall moment. Ask yourself, what is really going on in your character's universe at the moment your scene begins.

When is this moment in time?

Once you have established what the true moment is, then address the question is "***when***"is it? Using the example described above, the moment can be described as morning, day, or night but more helpful would be the moment after I lost my job or late at night after I have been walking for hours, because I didn't know how I would tell you. It is literally the definition of ***"now."*** Once you understand this, you will know what to play. But also understand that ***"now"*** is constantly changing as the moment evolves.

Where are you? What is the space for your character?

Even though you may perform your monologue or scene in any number of nondescript spaces, decide for your character specifically where this moment is taking place. Is it a familiar place like at home that you control, or a public space that you do not control, such as on a bus, in an elevator, or on a podium in front of a thousand spectators? What is the space? Is it small and confined, larger than life or somewhere in between? Do not confuse this with the Dynamic of Performance (which is more concerned with the physical properties of the performance space) the ***"where are you"*** question addresses solely the reality of the character's universe rather than the performance space. Make specific decisions about the space your character occupies when they begin to move and speak.

How to play each moment as if it were a piece of a larger mosaic – and create "THE MOMENT AFTER"

Where are you going?

If your character is in a particular space at a particular moment, where will they go next? Is it somewhere specific? Create a concept of motion. Let your words in the scene and the physical life you have in the moments you create propel you to the next.

Everybody likes to know where they have been and where they are going

I am not asking you to predict the future. However, your character and the audience, in a larger sense, should have some idea about where your character is going intellectually, emotionally, physically and spiritually because of watching the monologue or scene-taking place. Everybody loves to peer into the future and know, if only briefly, what the next moment will bring. Even if you don't really have a clear-cut idea of all of it, give your character, and your audience a taste of what may come next. An audience member, will say, ***"Okay, I have watched and listened to this monologue or scene. Now, as a result of this monologue or scene what's going to happen?"*** Answer the question: ***"Now that this monologue or scene has taken place, this is what's going to happen next."*** You have to share with the audience your character's vision of what the next step will be. You take them along with you on your journey.

"What has happened during this journey?" After all that has been said and done, has your character changed? Has your character revealed something about themselves or another character? It may be a minute change, but it is a change, nonetheless. What happens next? You as the performer and your character have to answer the question: How has the universe changed and because of what occurred in the monologue or scene and what will happen next? You do not have to write new lines to your scene, but there has to be a sense that something will follow.

How do you play the moment after?

We have come full circle. Your character must have some resolve intellectually, emotionally, physically, and spiritually that connects to what is going on within their universe.

How do you show the moment after?

The way your character contemplates what has just occurred in the scene or how they react emotionally, or how they physically accommodate those changes. Your monologue or scene does not end when one of the characters utters the last line. It ends when the audience experiences the character's reaction to the last line. The audience wants a sense of the significance of what has transpired and a glimpse of what will be. That is what keeps them invested in your character. They want to know and be part of what is going to happen next. Your scene, even though it is a sample, should propel the audience forward and make them want to know what's going to happen next.

At the end of the classic film CASABLANCA (1943) the final lines of the film end this part of the story but also propel the audience into the future when Rick and Captain Renault walk off into the fog to join the Free French Army: ***"Louis, I think this is the beginning of a beautiful friendship."*** While the audience doesn't know everything that will happen, they do know that because of what has taken place that the world for these two characters will be different than it has been before.

How to begin a monologue or scene at an acting class or audition

You have done your preparation. Now it's time to present. For an acting class, you should be familiar with the space and hopefully have rehearsed in it several times. When you are called, you alone or with your partner, should quietly set up whatever elements, set pieces, or props you will need. If you are using any type of recorded music or sound effects, I strongly suggest doing a sound check in advance to make sure the levels will work. You may be thinking, use of music or sound? Isn't that a bit over the top for a scene in an acting class? Not really, just as long as it's not a seven-piece band. Sometimes a script may have a specific cue for music and the characters comment on the song within the scene. I've also had actors use recorded sound for background. I remember a scene brought to class from the play INHERIT THE WIND by Robert Edwin Lee and Jerome Lawrence, where the two main characters were sitting on a porch on a summer night. The actors chose to have the recorded sound of crickets playing in the background that made the scene seem very authentic. It was a simple sound cue that went a long way to creating a reality of the scene. Once you are ready to go, cue the teacher and begin. It's so important that you do not speak during the set-up about the scene. Things like how few rehearsals you had, that it was difficult to find time to work with your partner, or that you have been very busy at work have no place here. This is your time to perform, not to explain or complain. You may choose to introduce the monologue or scene in which you might want to say something about the play or film, who the characters are, and in what part of the story the scene takes place within the whole body of the work. You can also do a similar button at the end of the scene. In either case, when you are ready to begin, cue your acting teacher and start the monologue or scene. Once you begin, remember that your monologue or scene does not have to begin with a line of dialogue. It can begin with an action. When you do this, remember what we discussed the moment before. Let the beginning be a reaction to whatever occurred the moment before. Now let's talk about starting a monologue or a scene for an audition.

If you have been asked to do a prepared monologue or scene as an audition, it will likely be for a theatrical agent (theatre, TV and film) considering you for representation. If you have gotten their far, it means they like the way you look (your type) and now want to see what you can do with prepared material. You may have already given them your reel, which has all sorts of scenes in it, but they want you to come in and do either a monologue or a scene live. Most of the time, these types of monologues or scenes are done in the agent's office or conference room, so intimacy is often a consideration. When you enter the audition space, get a sense of the room. What is the energy level of the people inside? Where are they sitting? In front of you, on the side or both? How large is the space? What is the distance between where you will perform and the people watching you? What is the acoustic quality of the space? Where is the light and are there any seats or other set materials in the space? Adjust to any deficiencies on the fly. If it is a larger space like a conference room or even a stage, and there is an object in your way from a previous audition, it is okay to use it or move it out of the way. Try to make the space as accommodating for your performance as you can. Make the space your own as you create the universe of your character.

If you are required to talk to them before you perform or do a verbal set-up which might include the scene title and a little bit of background about the source material and setting, try to be as concise as possible. Try not to use words like ***"um" or "like"*** and don't comment on extraneous things like how heavy traffic was, that there was no parking, or how late you worked the night before. Instead, be very specific and state the name of the source material and a short summary of the source material that you are performing and what (if anything) is unique about it. You can prepare this in advance and memorize it as part of the overall presentation. If the situation calls for you to go right into your monologue or scene, take some time to create the universe that your character lives in. If there is a bit of conversation before you perform, make sure you allow adequate time to separate the reality of the ***"audition conversation"*** and the reality of the "***universe of the character"*** you are to perform. Don't be a ***good soldier*** and go instantaneously from an interview into a character. You will not totally achieve the transition and your performance will seem uneven and full of distractions. Before you speak, take a moment to let your character's universe surround you. However, please don't do warmups. Stretch out or lower your head toward the floor as you ***get into character,*** then suddenly face forward as the character in a totally different physicality. This caution may seem elementary, but I see actors do it all the time.

Remember, what we discussed earlier, that your prepared monologue or scene does not begin with your first line. It begins with the moment before the first line, which causes your character to say the first line. A scene can even begin with a physical action or the creation of an emotional or physical state by the character. If you are playing Romeo, ask yourself, what causes this character to say:

"My lips, two blushing pilgrims, ready stand

To smooth that rough touch with a tender kiss."

The answer is that he sees Juliet and immediately falls in love with her. He just doesn't speak those words because Shakespeare wrote them. There is an underlying moment that occurs before the lines are spoken that drives the character to speak those words. When your character speaks those first words, let them be a reaction to a previous intellectual, emotional or physical moment. This can be a previous moment in the play, film, or something the audience has not even seen. It is a moment in the life and universe of the character. How you play this reaction to a previous moment has all to do with your character's intellectual, emotional, physical, and spiritual connection. Ask yourself the question, what does my character ***"think"*** about this situation. How does my character ***"feel"*** right now and how does my character respond ***"physically"*** to this place and situation. And what are your character's beliefs about the nature of their universe and what is right and what is wrong? Once you have answers to these questions, you will have something to play with.

Where should I look or who should I look at when I perform a monologue or scene for an acting or audition?

This may seem like a silly question to pose in this book. However, it has been my experience both in acting class and when I was an auditioner that actors would constantly break the reality of their scene to look directly at me. The reason for this may be that they want some sort of connection to the acting teacher or auditioner, or they may simply want to see how they are doing. In either case, this is not a good choice to make for several reasons. You shatter the reality you are trying to create for your character and more importantly, you are putting your acting teacher or auditioner in the awkward position of having to acknowledge you instead of making notes on your scene. If you are thinking about doing a monologue or scene, which is presentational, where you interact with and acknowledge the audience looking at them might be okay. However, I don't recommend a presentational type of scene for an audition. Casting directors or agents, for the most part, don't want to be part of your scene. You are there for an audition and this means you must allow them the space to watch and make notes of your performance. If you do acknowledge the audience, select a certain person or areas of the space to address rather than talking literally over their heads to some random spot. Some acting teachers direct their students performing monologues to speak ***just above the heads*** of their audience. I don't like this practice because it is distracting to watch and does not allow the person performing the most effective method of connecting the audience to your character. I think a better choice would be to interact with the other character in the monologue or scene as if the audience were not present. Make the universe of your character separate from that of your acting class or audition. Ultimately, I am not one for rules, if you perform your monologue or scene and acknowledge the auditioner, you will not fall through a hole in the floor. You can do anything you want to do to create the best reality for your specific presentation.

How do I end a monologue or scene at an acting class or audition?

In a typical production setting, when a monologue or scene in a play is over, the lights might fade and come up on another part of the stage or another character might speak in a different area of the stage. In a film, another character can speak; they could cut to the next scene or fade to black. In an acting class or audition setting, you will not have the same control over the space in which you will perform. You will not be able to end your monologue or scene with a slow fade of the lights or as in film cut to the next shot. Also, there may be harsh lighting; exterior noise, or it may not be a performance space at all. I have seen several methods of ending a prepared monologue or scene for an acting class that I suggest that ***you not do.*** The first one is at the end of the presentation. The actors just bow their head toward the floor as if to say, ***"it's over – you can applaud now."*** As you can imagine this unnatural ending is abrupt and solicits what may be artificial applause and response from your intended audience. Natural unsolicited applause belongs in a live theatrical performance. You may get natural unsolicited applause in your acting class and that is fine as long as it is not solicited. The second method that you should not do is at the end of the end of a monologue or scene when one or more of the actors say the word ***"scene."*** This is a verbal cue spoken out loud to the acting class or auditioner, indicating that the scene is over. This method is also unnatural and creates an abrupt, almost jarring ending. I've seen one actor in a scene exit and the other remains on stage, taking a moment when the off stage the voice of the other actor is heard saying ***"scene."*** This gives the scene an unnatural ending. Additionally, actors who use this method of scene ending tend to physically comment upon their work when they say ***"scene."*** They complete a scene and then, in a very different physicality, look up at the acting teacher or auditioner shrug upward in apology, and say ***"scene."*** This is not an ending; it is an apology. It is as if the actor says to the acting teacher or auditioner, ***"I'm so sorry for making you sit through this awful scene."*** All of these artificial methods don't allow the scene to end naturally. What then, should you do?

If we operate on the assumption that you are not directly addressing your acting teacher or auditioner during your scene, then ending your monologue or scene is very simple. You complete the last line or action and then allow a moment after to occur. This allows both the audience and if you have a scene partner to react to that last moment. You take this short beat, then change your physicality from the characters in the monologue or scene ***back*** to your own or neutral position and look directly at and acknowledge the acting teacher or auditioner. This will tell them that the reality that was created for the monologue or scene has now ended and that you are back at the in the class or audition. You don't ask for applause or any reaction for that matter. If the audience in the acting class or auditioner wants to applause, they can, but it will be a natural reaction to what you have created.

All you are communicating to the acting teacher or auditioner is that the monologue or scene is now over. Let them decide how they want to react. The acting teacher may at that point ask you questions and give you notes on your performance. They may even ask you to repeat certain portions of the scene to illustrate a choice. The auditioner normally will say ***"thank you"*** and that is it. They may comment on your performance, give specific notes, or ask you additional questions. Remember; don't comment on your performance because it is a losing proposition either way. If you say, ***"Wow, that was terrible. I can't believe how bad that was."*** They may not have felt that way. Alternatively, if you say, ***"Wow, was that hot or what? I can't believe how well we just nailed it today."*** In this case, they may also not agree. Best bet is to not comment at all and let them do the talking. If an auditioner asks that you perform portions again and provides notes, listen to them carefully and try to incorporate them into your second performance. Many times, an auditioner will give notes just to see how you take direction and incorporate their comments into your performance.

"

I graduated from school for graphic design, and I started to get into acting class just to get over severe fright. I was an extremely shy person. I could barely say hello to anybody.

"

Trevor Donovan

CHAPTER 10

How to Prepare for a Scene Assignment?

Selecting a scene partner for an acting class assignment or audition?

All actors should also be producers. The person who you choose to work with within your scene should be selected carefully on several levels, both for an acting class and for auditions. Think like a producer and pick the appropriate person to work with:

Character type

You want to select someone who is the right character "type" for the characters in your scene. The character type has to do with the appropriate age range, physicality, and demeanor (energy/outward energy) for the character in the play or film scene. If you have a limited group of students within your acting class, try to pick material that generally fits both of your age ranges. Many acting scene books that are used in colleges have many of the classic plays like Chekov, Ibsen, Brecht, or O'Neil, where the characters are older than the 18-23 demographic for college students. Students are forced to play characters older than they really are and, more importantly, characters they will never play professionally for decades. I am not saying that actors should not learn the classics, but it becomes an exercise in futility to have a twenty-year-old play a sixty-year-old. Yes, with talcum powder and wigs we can do it, but it really serves no learning purpose for the actor. So, try to select a scene that generally fits your age range and if you can, your physicality and demeanor.

In an audition, the casting of a prepared scene is just as important as an acting class with one other addition to character type. If you are doing a prepared scene as an audition for a talent agent, you will want to pick a scene partner that is a different acting type than you are. I cannot tell you how many times actors have asked their friends to do a scene with them for an agent and the friend who is the same gender and casting type gets the agent instead of the actor who had the appointment. I recommend trying to pick mixed gender or mixed age range scenes so that both actors can be considered and they are not competing for the same client spot in the agency.

Talent, skills, and commitment

Most acting classes have class members that are the stars within the micro universe of the class. They are the sought-after people that everyone wants to perform scenes with because of their looks, their talent or the success of their previous work in the class. In an acting class, of course, you want to select someone to work with that has a demonstrated track record of success. This type of person will do the required work, show up to rehearse, and be a true partner in getting the scene up on its feet. You don't want to have a scene partner that has a poor reputation in the class or one who isn't available to rehearse. You must also consider their commitment to the class. Some students take an acting class and literally take up space. They do very little work in class and generally do not contribute to the growth of their classmates. Stay away from these types of people because they will bring you down to their level instead of you bringing them up to your level. If you have any doubts about a person you have selected, talk to them. If they are not available to talk or don't answer your communications, discuss what is happening with your acting teacher and make a change.

This becomes paramount in an audition setting. If you are doing a prepared scene for an audition, you want someone who is prepared to put in the work in that needs to be done to achieve a positive result.

A reason ***"not"*** to pick someone to work in a scene with you.

Dating?

You select someone you want to date. Some students love to hang out in class and pick people to work with that they think they want to go out with. It rarely works because these people rarely want to do any of the work needed to do the scene and are usually dropped from the scene and the class.

How do I rehearse a scene for an acting class or audition?

1.Meet with your partner and select a scene and set up a specific rehearsal schedule up and including the due date. Exchange contact information.

2.Read through it for content and make cuts if needed

3.Come up with a collective point of view to present the scene.

4.Each person should make a list of props, costumes and set requirements - you can do this by setting up column space on each side of the script and making notations as you read through it.

5.Get it on its feet - either block in advance or sketch out a rough blocking set and let your character move through it. Once a pattern is established, you can set it. Also make note of any "physical business" such as fights, dance-type sequences - these must be set in advance.

6.Set specific goals for your character - set them out on the scene sheet included in your syllabus. Make sure you know the following:

What does my character want in the total scene?

Break the scene down into beats and set sub goals for each beat which lead toward the total scene goal.

Where has my character come from just before the scene?

Where is my character going or what has changed because of the scene?

Lastly, think about -

Intellectual - What does my character think about this situation?

Emotional - How does my character feel about this situation?

Physical - How does my character move and experience the space in relation to other characters or objects in the space?

Spiritual – What are my character's beliefs and values?

Work together and come to a consensus on how the scene will be presented.

What if the script is too long? Some ideas on editing

Read the entire piece out loud with feeling. Time the length of your reading. Subtract the allotted time the piece should be from your timed reading. Do not be afraid to "cut" all the extraneous material--even if you like it--the audience will not know it was there. Decide on the main thought or theme that goes through the scene. Remember that the purpose of the scene is to show your character. Cut off all extraneous material that does not fit into what you have decided for your character. Give the lines of one character to another and cut the character if the character is unnecessary to the plot line. Read piece aloud at the end of the cutting session to time it. Follow this procedure until the "cutting fits the allotted time."

Also, when doing a film script, you may have to combine several portions of a single scene together that would have been separated by time or location. You many have two characters at one location talking, then the script may cut away to something that is happening elsewhere and then cut back. Scenes can also be cut because of flashbacks or time cuts. Don't be afraid to edit the appropriate pieces together to give the scene a more complete feel. Caution, when doing a film scene, don't feel you are obligated to do exactly what is in the film. Remember, you are now acting in the scene and choices should center on what you and your partner are trying to achieve rather than what might be contained in a film that has already been shot.

Performance versus in class scenes:

Creating a point of view:

In a performance setting you will have a director to guide you through the process. A good director will normally state a point of view for the film or play. That is state the manner and direction in which they intend to present the material. For example, Romeo and Juliet can be presented in a traditional manner with costume and setting of the period implied by Shakespeare (Franco Zeffirelli) or modernized as in the version directed by Baz Luhrmann. The Point of View is how the director chooses to present the material. In a class presentation, scene partners must derive a point of view for their presentation and experiment around that agreed upon idea. The point of view should be established before the actual rehearsals begin so that both actors are focused upon one presentational goal.

Experimentation during rehearsal – try new things, then make specific choices

During experimentation, you will discover that not all choices work. Keep the choices that work for you and discard what does not work. Remember, you cannot play all things in one performance. Play your character moment to moment and become a reactor. Listen and feel and respond accordingly. Experimentation is part of the creative process. However, at some point specific choices must be made and then incorporated into the final presentation.

Creating a character and breaking down a scene:

What should you ask yourself when creating a scene either with a scene partner or as part of a professional performance?

Creating a Character

Remember what we have stated earlier. After reading the play or screenplay several times, make the following notes about your character. If you read the entire script (and you should) how are the three "P's" answered about your character?

Personal:Are they married, single, divorced? Live alone?

Professional:What do they do? Are they a doctor, lawyer, or spy?

Private:Some secret about your character that only they know. For example, a war hero who is really (privately) a coward.

Reading the Script

What does the writer say about my character?

How does the writer describe your character when they are first introduced to the audience?

What does my character do that is revealing about their personality?

How did they enter space when first introduced?

What does my character say about themselves?

Does your character ever speak about themselves in the form of a description or telling of some experience?

What does my character do?

What are your character's actions within the universe of the play or film?

What do other characters say about your character?

How do the other characters in the story describe your character? Do their descriptions agree or disagree with your own character's description of themselves?

How do other characters react when your character enters the space?

Do they react in a certain way or not react at all?

Breaking down a scene (Units or Beats)

Macro: Create an objective for the entire piece.

Look at the entire play or screenplay and create a **super objective** for your character within the entire piece. This can be stated regarding "My character wants... by the end of this play or movie." This could be a simple phrase: *My character wants to be a real boy* – Pinocchio, or *My character wants to get his boat back* - Jack Sparrow in Pirates of the Caribbean.

Micro: Create Objectives for each scene

Make a list of each scene your character appears.

How does that scene fit into the overall macro-objective?

What is your character's objective within each scene?

What are the barriers in that scene, which have to be overcome to meet that objective?

*Note: In Live Theater you may hear the term **FRENCH SCENE** - this is a term that refers to your character's objectives or central purpose between each entrance and exit.

Units or beats:

Within a scene, creating smaller divisions within the body of a scene. Each beat or unit should be tied to a particular physicality or piece of business. You may create smaller objectives within each beat or unit. Example: This could be a small section of a scene in which a character sits at a window seat and ponders their future. Once you have created your list, ask yourself the following questions:

1)Who will be in the scene? Which characters? The point of view character needs to present.

2) Where is it taking place? In a living room, a restaurant, in a car?

3) When? What is the time of day, season, year, etc.?

4) What is happening? Is there a problem? Are they just talking? Drinking coffee or a beer? Is someone pacing?

5) Why are they there? Invited to dinner, barged in, or sneaked in through the servant's entrance and are eavesdropping?

6) What are the motives of the other characters and how are they involved in your character's objectives. Are they supportive or do these serve as an obstacle? Are they suspects, victims, or witnesses?

7) What has just happened the moment before and what is about to happen?

For each question you can use the five senses to take notice of all the little things, that will be the windows in which your character senses the world around them.

Primary and Secondary Characters

A word about PRIMARY and SECONDARY characters in a scene. **If you are the pizza delivery boy and you have one scene in which you deliver a pizza. Just deliver the pizza.** This is just a random sampling of sample objectives. You can look up additional ones in a dictionary or thesaurus.

Create your own objectives

Actions, intentions, goals, or needs refer to an inner drive, something your character needs to do to, or wants to get from another character. It is essentially what you "act." You create a drive that causes the character to do and say things aimed at getting what they want. Just as in life all our words and behaviors stem from what we want from the people around us, needs or objectives likewise drive our characters.

During a play or movie, a character's dramatic through-line is made up of behaviors that are propelled by need.

"There is something I want, and I take this action,

I observe your response to evaluate if what I am doing and saying is working.

I adjust my actions based on your response,

I will try again."

It is a continuous, unbroken thread that, as an actor, you connect to each time you go the play or scene begins. Every moment of your performance, your character should be focused on achieving an objective.

How to have fun in an acting class or audition

This last note will sound strange and a bit cliché' but if you are having a good time, your acting teacher and auditioner will be more likely to become engaged in the intellectual, emotional, physical and spiritual life of the characters you create. Acting classes by their very nature should be enjoyable experiences. However, many students find the criticism they get there too personal in nature. Often there is an underlying insecurity in what they do that goes beyond simple criticism of their acting abilities. We all have individuals around us that support us and then we also have others that tear us down. In my classes, I always couch my criticism with praise by saying something the student has done well and then what they need to work on. I was a guest in an acting class one evening where the acting teacher berated the student's physical appearance and acting ability. That's not my style. So how to make an acting class fun? Answer: Enjoy the journey and don't make it personal. Make it a game that you play and enjoy, but one that is separate from what you do when you go home at night. Yes, an acting career is challenging and requires a lifelong commitment. However, it's only part of your life and who you are. If you get one of those drill sergeant type of acting teachers, drop the class if you find that type of criticism bothersome. On the other side of the coin, some students want intense negative and personal criticism.

Attending an audition is similar to an acting class because you are also judged. However, the very nature of an audition is selection for a particular project. It is and should never be personal. Always remember, an audition is a presentation for a creative project at a specific moment in time. Once that audition is over, let it go. Have no vested interest in it, put it behind you and forget it. If you got it they will contact you, if you didn't, there will be another one tomorrow. If you are doing a prepared scene for an agent, they are looking at you in relation to the other clients they already represent. If you fit a space in their client list, you will be selected for representation. If there is a conflict, you will not. I always have believed that the universe wants to provide great things to us... but we often hold on to the lesser things because we are afraid. My advice for a fun audition? Let go! However, it turns out, just have a great time doing it and remember why you wanted to be in actor in the first place. If you feel good about what you are doing, you will do it better. Can you visualize that first moment you had the thought that you wanted to be an actor? Maybe you were watching television, a movie, or a play. You sat in your seat, and you thought to yourself.

"I can do that! I want to be up there on the screen or on the stage. I want to do it because it's something I enjoy. No, it's something that I love. I love to act because it's inside of me and part of who I am. I can't think of doing anything else!"

Okay, so that seems a bit over the top. But didn't you ever feel this way, at least a little bit. Well, I want you to go back to that personal moment for you. Go back to it and remember that you wanted to act because you love it and it makes you happy when you do it. Keep that always in your heart and find joy in what you do. Even if you don't get the part or you get it wrong, it doesn't matter because there will always be another day, another audition and another part to play. Whether it's an acting class or an audition, have a great time. Be thankful that you can perform and share your talent. This is not really advice. It's common sense. But it goes to the core of why we act. We act because we love to act, and that passion should be part of everything that we do.

“

In acting class, teachers talk about how the 'givens' of a situation help define a character.

“

Hill Harper

CHAPTER 11

Auditioning
Cold Readings, Headshots and Resumes

An entire book could be dedicated to this subject, but I wanted to briefly go over it because many acting classes, especially those offered by colleges, don't discuss it at all. Why? Most college classes follow a specific set of learning objectives which are required by the school at large. I have always found it difficult for students to pay large tuition costs., take classes and then when their studies are complete, have no idea or training on how to apply with they have learned in a professional environment.

Cold Readings and Auditioning

As a professional actor you will be required to audition for specific roles in a television show, motion picture or live theatre production performing pages (sides) from a specific script. Also, mostly in theater, performers have a prepared monologue (comedy/dramatic), which can be used for auditions. Monologue material is presented memorized with a prepared beginning middle and end. However, in a television, motion picture or commercial audition, performers perform specific characters from pages from the full script. This is called a cold reading and is performed with the pages in hand.

Cold reading can be done both face to face and online and requires the ability to create a believable performance while still holding the pages of a script in your hand. Pick up a sample script and scoop up the first line by looking down at it and quickly committing it to memory. Then look up and say the line aloud. This, in essence a cold reading. Get used to capturing lines of dialogue. The more you do it, the better you will get at it. Next step is to practice it with someone responding to your lines.

Now that we have discussed reading the lines aloud cold, I want to say that the practice of cold readings as it exists today with technology is no longer cold. When performers have an audition, sides are available online in advance so they will have ample opportunity to download and memorize them. You will still hold the pages when auditioning as if you were reading it cold. The difference is, you should already be familiar with the material and can relate specifically to the other character you are reading with. Reviewing the pages in advance also provides you with the opportunity to listen and react to what is happening in the scene. How you listen to the other character is just as important as how you speak your own lines. You can refer to the pages you are holding from time to time. but most of your audition will be focused off the page relating intellectually, emotionally, and physically to the other character.

Try not to speak your character's lines while looking at the script. If you do, get the script at the reading, and have not memorized it, try to take the time, go over the script entirely at least once, and make choices. The essence of the character is_more important than_reciting the lines exactly as they are written. Hold your sides low and avoid waving the script around or using it as an extension of yourself or a prop. Don't put the script down even if you know all the lines. You want to give the impression that your performance is fresh and unrehearsed rather than fully prepared to give the impression that with more time, direction, and preparation the performance will only get better.

Face to Face or Online Auditions

Be friendly. Don't criticize the script or the project or yourself. Don't say anything about how "bad" you thought your performance was. Just show the casting director confidence and enthusiasm. Once the audition is over it is over, say "Thank you..." and leave or wait for them to end the session if it is online.

Be Specific: Make specific choices that are clear. Don't play everything. Everything will get you nothing.

Don't Apologize Don't Congratulate Yourself Ever: Don't comment on your performance ever. Don't say "Wow... that was terrible." Or "Wow, that was really good. I constantly amaze myself."

If there is conversation, let the casting director do most of the talking: Remember, an audition is just like selling. Sell yourself playing the role, but allow the casting director to talk about themselves through you. Don't just rattle off your credits and talk about how great you are for the part. Instead, seed your conversation with questions that allow them to talk about themselves or the project they are casting. Acknowledge them and listen.

Direction: Don't expect them to direct you. However, if they do, make sure you understand what they are asking you to do. Often a casting director will give a specific direction to assess how the actor takes direction. If they say something you don't understand ask for clarification. If they ask you, to make a choice you don't agree with, don't argue your interpretation with them, just try to do what they ask.

Ending your audition:

Saying "Scene" or "Bowing Your Head:" Avoid saying "Scene" or "Bowing your head" when you are done. Most of the time you can change your physicality to a neutral position and make eye contact with the casting director. That gesture says, I'm done. We will go over this in class.

Note if it is an online audition, don't sabotage yourself with poor technology. Make sure your sound and lighting are not distorted. If you evolve into doing many online auditions, invest in a halo light and high-quality microphone or lavalier clip on.

The Business of Acting – To get started you need two essentials

To function as a professional actor, you will be required to develop materials which you will need to help you to get auditions and eventually work.

Headshots

You need at least one good color or black and white headshot which reflects your personality and appearance. It is essential that the head shot be a representation of how you look. Your headshot should be a reasonable representation of your age, physicality, and demeanor. Many actors have several headshots accenting different aspects of their look and personality. All head shots must be in crisp focus and done professionally. Avoid taking a head show with your cell phone and make sure it is formatted for all digital casting formats. A professional headshot photographer will usually format your final selection of headshot to several digital formats as well as for 8x10 hard copy printing. Your headshot can be uploaded to various casting websites and used by you and an agent for audition submissions.

Resume

All professional actors must have an acting resume, which is a listing of their physical attributes, training, and acting credits. Remember that an acting resume is quite different from a regular employment resume that you might use to get an office job. It will not contain your personal home address, non-acting employment history, age, or social security number. See the example below:

Name

Your or Agent Contact Phone Number with area code

(SAG/AFTRA, EQUITY) if applicable

Eyes: Blue	**Height: 5' 8"**	**Hair: Brown**

THEATRE:

IT'S A WONDERFUL LIFE	George	USC School of Drama
DRACULA THE MUSICAL	Igor	Dark House Theatre
LITTLE DOG LAUGHED	Mitchell	Creative Center at West
ROMEO AND JULIET	Featured	Beverly Hills Playhouse

TELEVISION AND FILM

ESPN WORLD SERIES PROMO	Baseball Fan	ESPN Sports Television
BLUE BLOODS	Officer Sweeney	CBS Television
KILLERS IN THE ATTIC	Dr. Anthony Beckman	AFI Film - Lead Role

TRAINING:

USC School of Dramatic Arts	Scene Study/ On Camera	Frank Catalano
San Diego State University	Acting Film and TV	Lalo Stiles
UCB IMPROVISATION	Improvisation	Andy Goldberg

SPECIAL SKILLS:

Singing: (Soprano – and range)	Dance (Tap, Hip Hop, Ballet)	Improvisation
Dialects (Irish, Italian)	Language: Spanish	Soccer
Great with Animals	Instrument: Flute	Sky Diving
Martial Arts: Kung Fu	Motorcycle Riding	

(List of Commercials available upon request)

Note that this sample three column resume does not contain age or weight. Some performers indicate their age and weight range on the top, but your headshot should indicate your age range or physical weight. Most online casting sites will format your acting resume for you after you enter the information. Remember that an acting resume is a living document that will evolve as you add training or acting credits. If you choose to create a hard copy version of your resume to submit with a headshot, don't print the resume onto the back of your headshot. Instead, use a separate page cut to 8 x 10 and place it on the back of the photo.

Everyone has to start somewhere

As you get started as a professional actor, if you do not have credits, you can insert a general statement in place of credits, followed by training and Skills as indicated below.

I am currently studying acting (INSERT YOUR SCHOOL) taking classes including Scene Study, Monologue Preparation, Cold Reading Techniques, On Camera Acting and movement for actors. In addition, I am a member of our school's debate team. (Insert activity)

My theatre scene work includes:

Juliet from Romeo and Juliet

Helen from the Miracle Worker

George from It's a Wonderful Life

Kate from Kiss Me Kate

Follow this paragraph with training and skills in three-column format.

TRAINING:

USC School of Dramatic Arts	Scene Study/ On Camera	Frank Catalano
San Diego State University	Acting Film and TV	Lalo Stiles
UCB IMPROVISATION	Improvisation	Andy Goldberg

SPECIAL SKILLS:

Singing: (Soprano – and range)	Dance (Tap, Hip Hop, Ballet)	Improvisation
Dialects (Irish, Italian)	Language: Spanish	Soccer
Great with Animals	Instrument: Flute	Sky Diving
Martial Arts: Kung Fu	Motorcycle Riding	

The paragraph format is a great way to get your started and should be replaced as you obtain actual credits.

Other things to consider down the road

Acting Reel

As you develop more credits, you will be able to obtain a cut which can be placed on an acting reel. Your acting reel is a digital collection of samples of your work and should not contain full performances. Instead, you will include highlights of roles you have played in television and film. It should not be longer than three or four minutes. You can upload your reel or samples to most casting website. An acting reel like a resume, should be kept up to date as new credits are made available. Make sure that the production quality of its content is professional. Many on camera acting classes offer digital copies of work done in class, but these samples often have poor sound, lighting, and visual quality. It's better to use only those clips which come from actual credits. Also, note, that voice actors also create reels which are professional clips from the various types of voice-over projects they have done.

Acting Web Page and social media:

The internet is an excellent marketing tool for promoting your acting career. Creating a web page, Facebook, Instagram, or Tick Tok presence is a great way to let people know what you're working on and synergize with other actors in the industry. Your internet content like all other aspects of your career, must be kept current.

What About Talent Agents and Managers?

As you start your professional acting career, your focus should be on developing credits and getting experience. This is not to say that an acting agent or manager would not represent you as a beginner, but it is more likely they will want someone with some training and experience. The goal for you is to find representation that will actively seek opportunities for you. Many small agencies take on many clients and then submit them in bulk for projects. Casting directors will not ferret through a large submission of actors. They want your agent to select only those clients that are right for the role being cast. If you focus on credits, you will be able to get a better agent and ultimately more opportunities. Agents and managers are entitled to a percentage of your earnings, usually 10-20% and will only make money if you work. If you are approached by a representative that wants you to pay an upfront fee of any kind, do not do it. Sometimes companies will want upfront fees for classes and then promise guaranteed employment opportunities. These are usually scams. Guaranteed employment opportunities are provided by them by registering you in an "extra or atmosphere" casting service. You will be able to work as an extra but being an extra on a film set is putting your acting career on the fast track to nowhere.

Once you have enough credits, you have a choice of working with several types of agents and managers.

Commercial Agent – these agents will submit you for work in commercials.

Theatrical Agent - These agents will submit you for work in Television or Film.

Voice Over Agents - these agents will submit you for work as a voice artist.

Stage Agents - these agents will submit you for work on stage

One or several agencies may represent you for different types of work. You might have one commercial agent and another for theatrical. Often commercial and theatrical agencies can represent you for both within one company. Check out the specific talent agencies in your geographic location for representation. Voice-over agents should specialize in VO and should have an inhouse ability to record your auditions. Voice-over is a very specialized field and there are agencies that focus just on that. Check out the Voice Over Guide online for a list of current agencies. https://voiceoverresourceguide.com

Acting Managers:

Acting managers often work with one or more agencies on your behalf. An acting manager should focus on all facets of your acting career, developing a strategy toward specific goals. Acting managers are entitled to commissions of 10-20% outside what is payable to an agent. They can obtain auditions on your behalf but often work with agents in getting you specific jobs.

Acting as an Art and Business

If you choose to pursue a career as a professional actor, you must develop a strong work ethic, be organized, and have a passion for the art and drive to learn your craft. As you get started you also need to develop methods that ensure you have financial stability. This means you have to be able to pay your bills, put gas in your car and food on your table. If you live in a large city such as New York or Los Angeles, you must be prepared to address the higher cost of living. The hardest choice for most actors is to be able to work and earn money while still being able to be available to audition. Actors, like any business, should develop a steady source of income which financially supports their career efforts. This is important because they must have money to live day to day but must have funds to allocate to their acting career. Controlling the stream of funds and budgeting will ensure a solid financial base for them to build a career on. Must also develop a secondary income stream that they have total control over, in addition to solid financial management (month-to-month budgeting, a savings plan, investing in retirement as soon as possible, spending less than you make, and creating an emergency fund). Actors starting must have a side job that is flexible, such as a food server, temporary work, ride share, or online service. Remember, these positions are not your career. They are to fund your career.

Work Creates Work

Not all acting opportunities are traditional paying acting jobs! Acting in student films and plays is a great way to gain both experience and exposure. Working on quality student films and plays is a great way to showcase your acting talent. For student films, you will generally receive free transportation, and food as well as copies of the film. For plays, you may receive a small stipend for transportation costs and "comp" tickets for invited industry guests. The important thing is to keep getting out there and keep being seen. The most important thing to remember, is you have to live while you are building your acting career. Make sure you can earn money to pay your bills while you build your acting career. It is an evolutionary journey that may take you to opportunities you could not imagine.

“

The only failure is not to try.

“

George Clooney

CHAPTER 12

Using Your Acting Skills Performing and in Life

Utilizing Your Acting Skills in Everyday Situations

Okay, you have taken an acting class, now it's time to get out there and start auditioning. But are more ways than auditioning to use these acting skills. You can use your newly acquired acting skills to act on your creative ideas. How many times have you had an idea with a value that was valuable, and you thought of putting it together, making something tangible? But then, time passes, and your wonderful idea is placed on the back burner and eventually forgotten. You might have a dream one night, or get an idea while eating breakfast in the morning or driving in your car and you think about it and visualize it in your mind. Then time passes, you are working or doing chores and your idea fades away and is forgotten. Several months later, online or on television, you see your very idea has been created by someone else. You say to yourself, "I thought of that!"

So, what happened? Maybe you saw it somewhere and it really wasn't your idea. The bottom line, you didn't do it because you got very busy doing all the stuff that life requires and didn't have time to develop it. That kind of rationale or explanation makes it possible to accept why most creative ideas are never developed. We all can come up with many reasons including the things we have to do in life that are necessities that keep us from the kind of creative things we dream about. The difference between your necessities and desires are often in conflict with one another. What we perceive as necessities invariably comes from the logical part of our personality and our desires and hopes from emotion. The requirements of what you need now will always win out over your desire for the future. Fear of criticism or failure also plays a large role in deflecting any new idea that we may have. This fear of criticism and failure accelerates in a group environment. You're afraid of failing or being criticized by your family, friends, the people you work with and your immediate supervisor. The result is that your idea is never explored, and everything stays the same. How can we change this way of thinking? Let's take a moment and look at creativity itself.

Creative doesn't mean that you must totally invent something new that didn't exist in the universe before. Everything has existed before and has been said before. It is your interpretation of the ideas within your universe and combining them with other ideas that creates something new. But how do you do that? How do you become creative in everything you do? The first thing I think you would want to look at is to do something new that you haven't done before, just to get your juices flowing and add more abilities for your acting career.

Learn something new:

Learn a new skill. For example, you might want to learn a new language, how to make a chocolate souffle or how to write a poem? It will stimulate your brain to view your universe differently and start creating new things. The skills you would learn in such a class would help you to communicate your creative ideas. Your imagination is going to drive everything you do and that's what takes us to the second step, creating something new.

Create something new

This can be something that you learn and now apply. Don't fall into the trap of forcing you to think that to create something, it must be brand new and never heard or seen before by anyone? You can take something that's already in existence and improve upon it. Try to look at preexisting ideas in a fresh way and combine them with your thoughts to create something new and different.

"Imagination is the beginning of creation. You imagine what you desire, you will what you imagine, and at last, you create what you will."

George Bernard Shaw

Don't be afraid of criticism or failure

Not all things or ideas we create are going to be great. Think about Thomas Edison. As an inventor, he tried to make an electric light bulb 1,000 times unsuccessfully. No matter how many times he tried and failed, he just kept going. He faced criticism and failure, but on the 1001st attempt he was successful. The important thing is he kept on trying and putting it out there for the world to see.

"Many of life's failures are people who did not realize how close they were to success when they gave up." "I have not failed. I've just found ten thousand ways that won't work."

Thomas Edison

Use acting skills to manifest your ideas into a tangible reality

It's time to get out of the box and present. Once you have a really good idea to share, lock it down in your mind, even if you must write it down on a piece of paper. Once you have it where you want it to be, then don't be afraid to announce it to your universe. Even if it is not totally complete, you, by communicating in this way, create ownership. You might be thinking if I announce it to the world, it might be stolen by someone else. I think the opposite. By announcing it you create ownership and at the same time motivation to manifest your idea into a reality. The most important aspect of creating an idea is to eventually move it from an idea it into something tangible and real.

Think about how you can use what you learn in an acting class to present an idea clearly to other people. Your newly acquired acting skills will make it easier to present your ideas. Remember, it's not enough to just create something in your mind; you must communicate that idea to others who will help you manifest it into something that is tangible and real.

"Whatever you can do or dream you can, begin it. Boldness has a genius power, and magic in it. Begin it now!"

Johann Wolfgang Von Goethe

Using Acting Skills to Borrow from an idea that already exists

In the early part of the twentieth century, a man named Frank Gilbreth observed the way construction workers and more specifically brick workers, performed their jobs. After studying their procedures and motions, Gilbreth came up with a more efficient way for them to do their job. Later he expanded his efficiency ideas and applied them to a larger concept of time and motion studies. He improved procedures for manufacturing, sports, and even perfected the way surgeons operated on patients. He devised a system having a nurse assist the surgeon during an operation by providing instruments upon request. The surgeon could focus on the procedure and simply say "scalpel" and the nurse would then provide the instrument without any time being lost. This creative idea was based on something that already existed. The only thing that changed was now there was a new way of doing it. Gilbreth improved upon a procedure that already existed. What about you? Is there anything at home or workplace that you can improve? Maybe it is the way certain things are done or you might invent something new. The most important thing is to use the skills that you learned in acting class to communicate this idea so that you can get what you want.

"There is no waste of any kind in the world that equals the waste from needless, ill-directed and ineffective motions, and their resulting unnecessary fatigue. "

Frank Bunker Gilbreth, Sr.

How do you get an idea started?

Now it's time for action. I want you to analyze your universe and think about things that you can learn from it that are either part of it or outside it. Taking an acting class has started you on a journey that will change your life forever. It's important for you to get a clear understanding of how you are perceived by the universe you inhabit. Use your acting skills like the ancient Greek Sophists did by communicating with the people around you. Every morning you open your eyes, and think about what you will create that day. Then do it!

Enhance Your Skills

You could learn a new language or dialect, take a dance or martial arts class, voice over or singing. Each of these would then be added to the skills section of your resume. You could also focus on skills that will help you that are not related to acting, such as using marketing, social media, or project development tools. If you work in the hospitality industry, for example, you might take a cooking class. I remember when I was a graduate student in Hawaii, I took a job as a condiment supervisor at the campus cafeteria. I thought this would be a great job for free food and a way to make money to pay my bills. I learned how to make in bulk Thousand Island dressing with mayonnaise and ketchup that I poured from a big vat, thickened with a hard-boiled egg pressed through a sieve, mixed with sweet pickle relish. I was only on that job for a short while when I was promoted to a food line supervisor coordinating activities in the kitchen and the distribution of food to the cafeteria line. That's a fancy way of saying I stood behind the food line and waited until a food tray ran out, and then I would simply yell through a small window to the back kitchen for a replacement. How did those two experiences in the food industry teach me skills that I would need as a graduate student studying Asian Drama? The truth is that my culinary adventure, as short as it was, had little or nothing to do with my major, but it opened my mind up to thinking a different way. I looked at the cafeteria and graduate school from a different point of view. I knew how it all worked and that influenced how I viewed the rest of the world. Did that new point of view really matter? Yes, it mattered because it was that my brain was functioning in a different way because I was doing something that I had never done before. This different point of view created the opportunity for me to think about and create something new.

Creating something new, inspired by what I learned at my cafeteria job, made me think of other things I had never thought of before. This new thinking inspired me to write new plays. It also inspired me not to be afraid and to try new things. I traded in my job as a line supervisor, and I got a television show instead as a voice actor. This was an entirely new skill for me, but I was not afraid to try. At first, when I got to the studio, I knew I would eventually learn and succeed. The cafeteria gave me the motivation to do voice over acting. I'm using that word motivation, which we use in theater for actors portraying characters, pointed me in the direction of something that was closer to what I wanted to do and felt comfortable with. The process never ends.

When you start something new, you learn it and then it inspires you to do another, even better thing. Once I started to do voices and master both live action and animated characters, with a new skill, a new opportunity opened for me. The television scripts for the television show were written in Tokyo, Japan and then sent to us for recording. These scripts were written in a literal English translation. Here's an example. Two characters meet on a bridge and their cars are both blocking the way forward. One of the characters screams: ***"Hey, move your car pal, or I will beat you to many pulps.***" That is the literal English translation from the original Japanese script. The English or slang translation would be ***"Hey pal, move your car or I'll beat you to a pulp!"*** We would have to rewrite lines like this in the studio, which took a lot of time. I began converting all the scrips from Tokyo into conversational English before we went into the studio. After a period, the producers dumped the Tokyo scripts and hired me to write them in conversational English from the start. This is an example of learning something new and then creating something entirely new and different from something that already exists. The conversational which I wrote, allowed the voice actors to record in the studio more efficiently. It was an improvement over an existing process. When you learn something new, don't be afraid of criticism.

When you put your ideas out there, either orally or in writing, you're going to get individuals that criticize them. My point here is you can't let criticism stop you from what you're trying to achieve. Also remember that your idea may not work. Your idea may not totally be a good one or it may need improvement. And that improvement can be obtained through collaboration or repetition until you get it right. Think of. Edison and his invention of the light bulb. He had to work on that singular idea over 1000 times until he got it right. I am sure along the way lots of people said he was a failure, but he kept going. That's the important thing that I wanted to share with you, that you keep going. It doesn't mean you have to stay with your original idea. You can amend it or evolve it so that it eventually becomes successful, and it works for you.

"Don't waste your energy trying to change opinions...Do your thing, and don't care if they like it."

Tina Fey

Once you decide to communicate your idea, this is where your experience in an acting class becomes essential because you're going to be more adept at imparting that idea to others. You're not going to be nervous or afraid to speak. You are going to clearly present your ideas and yourself and answer questions you might receive with confidence. If you don't understand the question, you will ask for clarification. In short, you will present yourself with self-assurance and clarity.

Let's not forget what you learned in acting class. You have created a character and this person lives in the universe of a play or movie. In your world, you have created a character, and that character operates within the universe of your work environment. I want you to think about that because you should consider how that character presents this idea? Don't forget that when you are making a presentation. If you are the confident, knowledgeable character at home or at work, and when you make a presentation or communicate an idea, you decide to become the "class clown." That's not going to work. It wouldn't work on stage or film, and it wouldn't connect in your reality. People listening and watching are not going to know who you are and will find it very uncomfortable relating to this new character. It's okay to use humor, but think about how the character you are portraying would use humor to communicate with an audience.

Online Presentations

You may be in a situation where your actual communications will not be face to face in a traditional setting and that you may be relegated to an online presence. But all the same rules of communication will apply. If you present online, think of this as your own television that you will produce. Create visual tension so that your viewers are connected to your ideas. Have some visual illustrations so that people are not just looking at you through a box on a screen. It's just like watching television to our brains and people want to have something to watch rather than just communicating with a talking head.

When you are making an online presentation. Remember what you've learned in your acting class, and that is, you're going to create a character. Create a physicality, a vocal quality, and a look directed toward the person that is going to be experiencing your idea. Let's remember what you learned in your acting class that your character must have physical, emotional, spiritual, and intellectual attributes. Once you have your character developed, think about dressing so that whatever people see of you, is professional.

Let's talk about technology, simplify whatever visual elements that you're going to use. You don't need a lot. It doesn't have to be overly visual, but you don't want to be just a talking head at the same time. Make sure you have prepared yourself technically by checking the sound and visual elements including background. I suggest that you use Bluetooth lavalier mic and you can purchase a ring light created for online presentations which you make look natural rather than washed out. Make sure you test before you go live. Record something and play it back just to make sure that you look, sound professional.

When presenting and idea or auditioning, remember your acting class. Don't forget to create a character that exists in a specific universe. This means I want you to create that universe by the way you dress and what is behind you when you are talking on the computer. You don't need to create a set or use a projected fake background. I would prefer just having a simple clean background which doesn't distract from what you're trying to communicate. Your background should be something bland or you can invest in a green screen. Don't forget background sounds children, people talking, phones, dogs barking, cats, meowing; all of that must be reduced and you must be in a quiet, focused environment.

Technology and Connecting

Make sure your Internet works well so that you are not prevented from communicating by slow or sporadic technology. When making a presentation or audition, it's just like you're in a play or a movie; you're going to connect your character to an audience, using the same techniques you would in an acting class. If it is a group presentation make sure you acknowledge each person by soliciting their participation. Ask questions that require them to provide answers. You can address the question to one of those people and then let that person respond so you have a bit more control and it's not rambling, once you get your idea across and it is fully communicated, don't forget to have a clear-cut ending which might open to audience questions. In Musical Theatre, when a song ends, there is something called a button. It is a method of letting the audience know the song is over and that they can applaud. Put a button on your presentation. Make them clearly know when it is over. You might say, thank you for listening, are there any questions? That's your way of telling them your presentation is over. Everyone wants to know when it's over so they can respond.

"

Life is like a play: it's not the length, but the excellence of the acting that matters.

"

Lucius Annaeus Seneca

Final Thoughts

If I can leave you with one last and final thought about Acting and Getting Started. It is to tell you to do it now. Don't wait until tomorrow because you have to fulfill some other obligation. Remember that you will always need to do something and that will prevent you from achieving your dreams Need will always take precedent over desires, and that very fact will prevent you from getting what you want. Also remember that your desires can evolve and it's okay to change. The most important thing is to keep moving forward, and not be afraid to communicate your dreams to others. It is only then that they will be achieved.

"

When you reach an obstacle, turn it into an opportunity. You have the choice. You can overcome and be a winner, or you can allow it to overcome you and be a loser. The choice is yours and yours alone. Refuse to throw in the towel. Go that extra mile that failures refuse to travel. It is far better to be exhausted from success than to be rested from failure.

"

Mary Kay Ash

Made in United States
Orlando, FL
10 December 2024

55335913R00098